An Introduction to Curriculum Studies

Philip H Taylor
University of Birmingham

Colin M Richards
University of Leicester

NFER Publishing Company

Published by the NFER Publishing Company Ltd.,
Darville House, 2 Oxford Road East,
Windsor, Berks. SL4 1DF
Registered Office: The Mere, Upton Park, Slough, Berks. SL1 2DQ
First published 1979
© P. H. Taylor and C. M. Richards 1979
ISBN 0 85633 164 3

Typeset by Yale Press Limited,
Carmichael Road, Norwood, London SE25
Printed in Great Britain by
Page Bros. (Norwich) Limited
Distributed in the USA by Humanities Press Inc.,
Atlantic Highlands, New Jersey 07716 USA.

Contents

Preface 7

Acknowledgements 9

1. *The Scope and Purpose of Curriculum Studies* 10
2. *Conceptions, Ideologies and the Curriculum* 25
3. *Curriculum Development* 47
4. *Curriculum Design* 63
5. *Curriculum Change and Innovation* 79
6. *The Curriculum in Operation and in Context* 109
7. *Curriculum Evaluation* 123
8. *Curriculum Theory and Research* 143

Index 160

Preface

Curriculum Studies is now established as an important component in the study of education. Increasingly it is being taken both by students training to be teachers and by teachers taking advanced courses. In its early years it was heavily influenced by work undertaken in the United States, but the sixties and seventies have seen the development of a distinctive British tradition addressing the particular concerns and problems of curricula in British schools. This book attempts an overall introductory perspective synthesising British work but also drawing on some American material.

It is a text-book, not a research monograph. It does not report many new findings nor does it present new conceptual analyses, but hopefully it does provide a fresh overall perspective which could prove useful to those attempting to find their way around this complex field of study. The book, deliberately short, does not seek to prescribe any one approach to curriculum research and development, but to put a great deal of diverse material into a new overall framework. The aim is to give students an initial 'sense' of the field of curriculum studies and a 'feel' for its concerns and complexities. By providing plentiful references and suggestions for further reading, it provides a springboard for further study and reflection rather than a definitive all-encompassing account.

The authors would like to acknowledge the help of a number of colleagues in commenting upon aspects of the book, especially Dan Wicksteed and Dick Puttock of Worcester College of Higher Education and Barry Abell of West Midlands College, (who also helped compile the index). Mrs Pam Cotton and Mrs Marcia Rosen need to be thanked also for their cheerful efficiency in deciphering handwriting, in correcting spelling errors and in typing the final manuscript.

Philip Taylor
Colin Richards
Birmingham and Leicester.

Acknowledgements

Grateful acknowledgement is made to the following publishers for figures used in this book:

Hodder and Stoughton Educational for figure 8 taken from Wheeler D., 1968, *Curriculum Process,* page 31

University of Chicago Press for figure 9 taken from Walker D., 1971, 'A naturalistic model for curriculum development', *School Review* 80,1, page 58

Peacock Publishing Company for figure 12 adapted from Stufflebeam D. *et al.,* 1971, *Educational Evaluation and Decision-Making,* page 39

Ward Lock Educational for figure 13 taken from Taylor P. and Walton J.(eds.), 1973, *The Curriculum: Research, Innovation and Change,* page 94

Macmillan Education for figure 15 taken from Taylor P. *et al.,* 1974, *Purpose, Power and Constraint in the Primary School Curriculum,* page 36

Chapter 1
The Scope and Purpose of Curriculum Studies

Introduction

Recent years have seen a great interest in what is taught in schools and what ought to be taught there. This interest has arisen for a number of reasons. There have been changes in society, in its attitudes and values. There have been moves towards greater social equality and away from social discrimination of all kinds, whether on the grounds of sex or colour or creed. Social relationships are now less constrained and less authoritarian than once they were. Alternative, and less conventional, ways of living together in society have become acceptable.

Changes in society and in people's views about what is permissible and what is not are only two areas of change which affect what people think should be taught in schools. Economic and technical changes also influence what people think the content of education should be. This century, developments in science and technology have been largely responsible for the rise in material prosperity which most Western countries have enjoyed, and on which they continue to depend. Because of this a knowledge of science and, very recently, technology has come to be considered as essential an ingredient in the education of most children as reading, writing and mathematics.

Science and technology have not only brought prosperity, they have also brought problems — problems of pollution and the potential destruction of the world in which we live. At the heart of such problems lie moral issues about how man should use his knowledge and the resources of the world in which he lives, and how he should treat his fellow men. 'Should we not teach the young how to confront such problems?' has been a question raised by many educationists in recent years. This has been behind the attempts to have social studies and moral education taught in schools, and has influenced the development of humanities courses[1].

Interest in the content of education, in the curriculum, is not, of course, simply a contemporary phenomenon. It has many historical counterparts. Over 2000 years ago Plato[2] was interested in what the leaders of an ideal state should be taught, and so have been many philosophers and statesmen since, when they came to consider the educational problems of society[3]. The reason for their interest is simple: the content of education, the curriculum, is at the heart of the educational enterprise. It is the means through which education is transacted. Without a curriculum education has no vehicle, nothing through which to transmit its messages, to convey its meanings, to transmit its values. It is mainly because of the crucial role which the curriculum plays in educational activities that it is worthy of study.

The remainder of this chapter aims to outline many issues which the study of the curriculum involves and to provide a basic 'map' to the areas covered in curriculum studies, areas which contribute to answering two fundamental questions: 'What is taught?' and 'What ought to be taught in educational institutions?'

What is the curriculum?

So far the assumption has been made that the terms 'curriculum' and 'the content of education' mean one and the same thing. This is a valid assumption if by the 'content of education' is meant the course of study to be followed in acquiring an education. This last is in fact the oldest known meaning of the word 'curriculum'. In contemporary writings, however, the phrase 'course of study to be followed' is frequently translated into 'the subjects to be studied' or 'the educational experiences to be provided', and not infrequently into the actual 'subject matter to be covered' (see Figure 1).

Figure 1
CONTENT OF EDUCATION—CURRICULUM

COURSE OF STUDY

EDUCATIONAL EXPERIENCES

SUBJECT TO BE STUDIED

SUBJECT MATTER

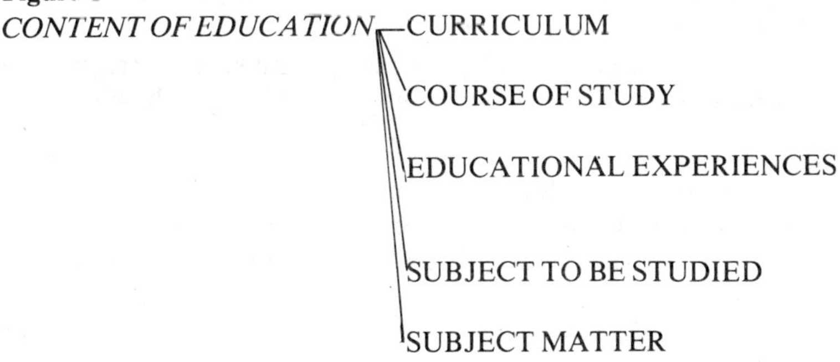

None of the terms, used to mean the content of education or the curriculum, is necessarily to be preferred to another. Very much depends on the context to which reference is being made. The nursery school does not have a curriculum of subjects but it does provide educational experiences through its painting corner, its sand and waterplay and the toys it makes available. Subjects come later in the secondary school where the curriculum may comprise eight or ten different subjects to be studied. It is also in the secondary school, and more so in further and higher education, that different courses of study are found — academic courses, vocational and practical courses. Provided the terms used to mean the curriculum are used with consistency and accurately reflect what content of education is intended, then no harm will have been done. It is only when there is disregard for the principles of consistency and accuracy that difficulties arise.

Problems of definition have, however, occurred in much writing about the curriculum for reasons other than failure to be consistent and accurate. Some writers have wanted to include within the meaning of the term 'curriculum' not merely courses of study or subjects to be studied, but all the activities deliberately planned for the pupil by the school[4]. Such activities arise not only from subjects or educational experiences provided by the school but also from the ways in which these are provided, from the form teaching takes, and from the 'milieu' or 'climate' created by the exercise of rules and regulations within a school. Such a definition of curriculum, though drawing attention to the fact that curricula are to be found in institutional settings in schools and colleges, makes for confusion with a term such as 'schooling'. This confusion can be avoided by the recognition that courses of study and educational experiences may be qualitatively affected by the settings in which they are to be found, and that subjects and subject matter may be given subtly different meanings by the way in which they are taught. The readiness to recognize the influence of setting and teaching on curricula will be examined more fully in Chapter 6.

Aims, objectives and the curriculum
Subjects studied and activities provided in schools are there for a reason. In the most general terms, they are there because it is believed they will serve worthwhile purposes and are likely to achieve intended and desired ends. An example of the reasons that

can be given for a curriculum appears in the upper school prospectus of an English comprehensive school:

> 'The subjects you study in the school are intended to give you a broad training in the different ways there are of learning, thinking and acquiring knowledge, so that you will have a basis for the future development of your mind, including your various skills'. (Pilton School, Devon, 1971)

The major purpose of the subjects to be studied is to provide *'a basis for the future development of your mind, including your various skills'*. The training in different ways of learning, thinking and acquiring knowledge is a means to this end. It is not the end in itself. The end is a basis for continuing intellectual development which is taken to include the capacity to exercise a range of relevant skills. The end or aim is not assured of achievement, of realization. It is what is hoped for, what is intended as the outcome of the endeavour.

From this example it is clear that the curriculum serves a purposive function which is broad in scope, and that constituent parts of the curriculum — subjects studied or activities provided — are the means through which worthwhile purposes may be achieved. The intended ends of studying subjects, the different ways of learning which they help to develop, the skills and capacities engendered by learning experiences, are the objectives of the curriculum. They are not the overall purposes or aims which the curriculum is intended to serve.

Much has been made of the distinction between the aims which the curriculum serves and the objectives through which the aims may be achieved, because of the very strong emphasis on objectives in much of the American literature[5]. When placed in the correct perspective, as means not final ends, curriculum objectives can be valuable aids in curriculum planning but only after the overall purposes of the curriculum are made explicit.

Teasing out the aims that a curriculum serves comes not from a consideration of the activities or subjects which comprise the curriculum but from a study of the reasons given for justifying the selection of subjects to be studied or activities to be experienced. In most cases the reasons are rooted in particular conceptions of education — in beliefs about what education is.

Conceptions of education and the curriculum

As has been pointed out earlier, views about what education is for are not fixed and permanent. They are subject to change and, because this is so, views of what should be taught in schools are also subject to change. At the beginning of this century the goal of education for the most of the population was universal literacy[6]. Today education aims at very much more even at the primary stage — at social, moral, aesthetic, physical, intellectual and 'personal' development[7]. Language and literacy have a role to play in the achievement of all these aims[8].

More than change is responsible for differing views of education. There are the beliefs, strongly held, about what aims education should serve. There is the belief that in essence education is the transmission of culture — the means whereby a society ensures the continuity of values from one generation to the next and so conserves itself[9]. A contrary belief holds that it is not the function of education to help conserve society but to enhance to the maximum the individual's potential. This last belief about the purpose of education permeates much of the Plowden Report[10]. There are other beliefs too, for example, the function of education in servicing the 'expert' society with skilled manpower. Beliefs such as these are outlined in the second chapter.

As Chapter 2 shows, these beliefs are related to other beliefs about the nature of society, childhood, learning and knowledge. Individual sets of beliefs have a good deal in common, and it is possible to group the multiplicity of such beliefs into a smaller number of educational ideologies — systems of meanings about education held by groups of people in society.

What has to be recognized is that it is these beliefs about the nature of education and its aims which set the context for decisions about what to teach, and even about how best to teach it (see Figure 3, p. 20). This is because beliefs about what education is encompass beliefs about what knowledge is, about knowing, about meaning and about how learning takes place.

For example one ideology prominent in primary education asserts that knowing is an active process in which the child must be caught up; that knowledge is what has meaning for the child at the child's stage of development; and that learning takes place by a process of exploration and discovery[11]. In contrast a very different ideology, especially dominant in traditional sixth form education, asserts that knowledge is organized in subjects; that knowing is the acquisition of the ordered information within these subjects; that meaning is acquired from an understanding of the principles which govern ways of ordering the information within specific subjects, and that learning takes place by submitting oneself to the discipline of the subject. Moreover, the best kind of learning is that which requires 'depth' and comes from the study of a few subjects[12].

Curriculum Development

In theory at least, the curriculum is developed from particular views as to what education is. In practice, beliefs about the nature of education are mixed — more a matter of relative emphasis than complete reliance on one view to the exclusion of others — and much a matter of habit and history. What was taught yesterday tends to be taught today unless conscious efforts are made to change it through developing alternatives.

The planning and creation of alternative curricula is what curriculum development is about. Its end products are a range of intended curricula comprising proposals for what ought to be taught in scholls (see Figure 3, p.20). The processes of curriculum development range from small-scale modifications of current practices to large-scale innovations in which new curricular possibilities emerge. The Schools Council and the Nuffield Foundation have funded at least one such large-scale curriculum innovation in the form of the Humanities Curriculum Project (see page 73). The development of this project began with a general point of view about what should be taught (in this case, in the humanities) and proceeded to develop the means to give these ideas a practical realization. This happens through the employment of some media; subject matter, for example, or, as in the case of the Humanities Project, 'evidence' on which to draw. This material becomes the focus of the teaching and learning of skills and capabilities, attitudes and values which are considered worthwhile in that they will lead to a better understanding of mankind's problems.

The development of new points of view about what should be taught is surrounded by contention. New curricular possibilities have to compete with already established assumptions about what should be taught and with what is already being taught in the schools. From the time when a new curricular possibility emerges to its implementation in the schools may be as long as fifty or more years[13]. It is also the case that some potential curricular innovations are never realized, as was the case with the movement to establish Citizenship as a subject in the secondary school curriculum[14].

The design of new courses, the assumptions underlying the activities of curriculum development and the factors influencing the success or failure of such activities are considered in Chapters 3, 4, and 5. Understanding the issues involved in activities concerned with curriculum development is a crucial area of curriculum studies. Without an understanding of the issues teachers remain at the mercy of events, of unnoticed assumptions, of unrecognized influences and of the prejudices of habit and practice. Equally important to an understanding of the processes of curriculum development is an understanding of what happens to intended curricula as they are worked upon in schools and classrooms. Some of the factors influencing the translation of intended curricula into operational curricula (what is actually taught) are examined in Chapter 6.

The Curriculum in Operation

It is only when the curriculum is enacted, given meaning through teaching, that it finally becomes a reality for pupils. It is through the operations of teaching and the learning which follows that intended curricula are realized (see Figure 3). However, between intention and realization there are many decisions to be taken and issues to be resolved, and there are many factors that constrain the best efforts of teachers to achieve the aims of the curriculum. At a self-evident level are the abilities of the children, their eagerness to learn, the support they receive from home. There are the numbers of children which a teacher has to manage, the physical conditions of school and classroom, and there is the skill and experience of the teacher. These factors and many more make the realization of the intended curriculum problematic.

At a less obvious level, the teacher's perception of what was intended by the curriculum developers and his ability to shape his teaching so as to facilitate the achievement of their intentions add to the difficulties in realizing the objectives and aims of the curriculum. It is in the unnoticed assumptions which teachers make about teaching and learning and in their habits and practices that the problem may have it roots. As an illustration, a study of middle

Figure 2. *The Elements of a Simple System.*

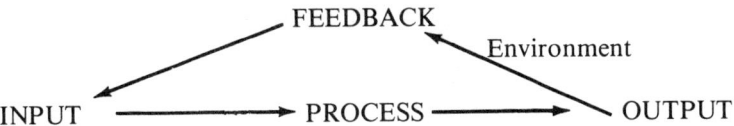

Each stage in a system's operation can be studied separately for the kinds of decisions and actions which are involved. A beginning for the major curriculum systems has been made in Figure 3 where the decisions and actions are given in terms of some of the questions which are answered in each system. Such a systems framework is *not* all-embracing *nor* can it be taken as a definitive model for curriculum studies. It does, however, provide an overall framework which helps give form and coherence to this field of educational study.

Curriculum theory and research

It is an oversimplification (but a useful one) to say that there are two kinds of curriculum theorizing, one drawing on the language of building, designing and constructing, and the other drawing on the language of politics, diplomacy and human relationships[18]. One type of theorizing sees curriculum processes as essentially technological enterprises, the other as essentially human enterprises. However, the oversimplification may serve a useful purpose in setting the limits within which theorizing about the curriculum takes place.

There are also two types of curriculum theory — prescriptive and 'scientific'. The aim of the first is to provide guidance for curricular practices. The aim of the second is to provide description, explanation, understanding and, if possible, prediction. The second takes curricular practices *as they are*. The first strives to move curricular practices toward *a desired pattern*[19]. Prescriptive curriculum theory draws on the findings of 'scientific' curriculum theory if it finds them useful. In turn 'scientific' curriculum theory may take prescriptive curriculum theory as an object of theorizing if it promises to enhance the understanding of what the curriculum is and how it comes about[20].

20 An Introduction to Curriculum Studies

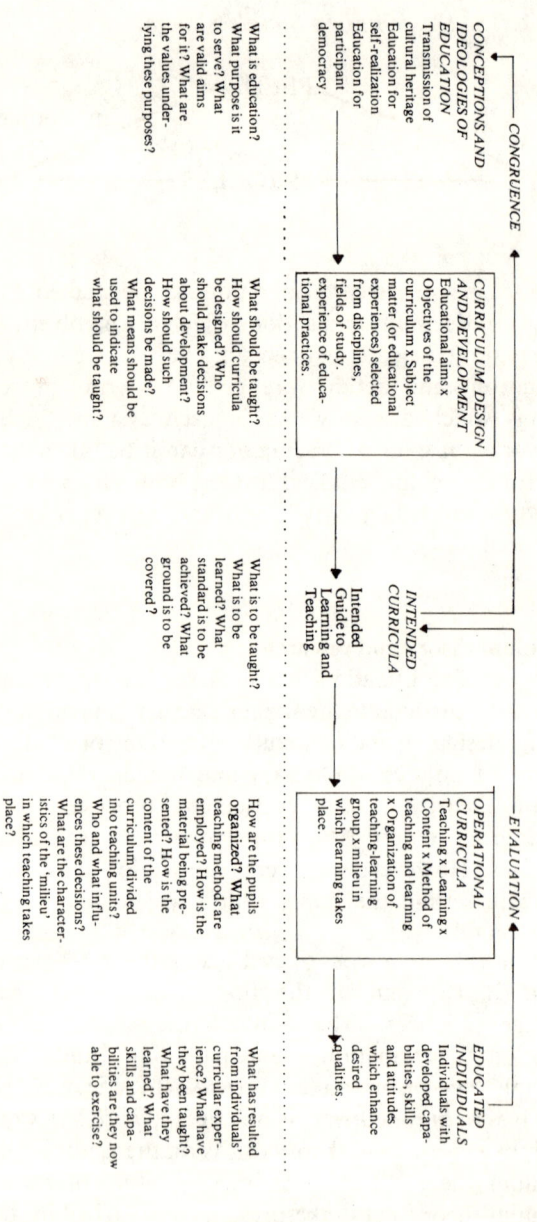

Figure 3. THE SCOPE AND CONCERNS OF CURRICULUM STUDIES: A TENTATIVE SYSTEMS MODEL

Whichever kind of theory and theorizing, there has to be an object of theorizing. For curriculum theorizing there are many objects and processes to theorize about:

1) Curriculum development
    change
    innovation
2) Curriculum operations
    influence
    constraints
3) Curriculum evaluation
    congruence
    appreciation
4) Curriculum materials
    equipment
    settings

and many sources on which to draw for the raw materials of theorizing. Curriculum research examines the phenomena of the field and provides empirical data for theorizing. Much research is drawn on in the chapters which follow and the more important areas for research set out in the second part of Chapter 8.

On the purpose of curriculum studies

This chapter has attempted to suggest the scope of curriculum studies and to point in a preliminary way to the questions that curriculum studies seeks to ask and to answer. Fundamentally, there are two major questions: 'What is taught?' and 'What ought to be taught in educational institutions?' Other questions are derived from, or are dependent upon, these. The chapter has, however, said only a little about the reasons which may be offered for studying the curriculum. By this stage many reasons may have occurred to the reader, and more may arise after reading subsequent chapters. Among the reasons are the following:-

1. The central role which the curriculum plays in the educational process makes it important that we should know as much as possible about how curricula come into being and function. Here the concern of curriculum studies is to improve our understanding of an important part of the educational enterprise.

2. The concern to improve the curricula of schools can be provided with practical backing from a study of the curriculum development and planning processes.

3. The need to monitor the effects of curricula can be better served by a clearer understanding of how curricula are intended to function and of the factors which affect their actual implementation.

For these and other reasons the study of the curriculum promises to be useful to teachers who have to enact the curriculum and to pupils and society whom it is intended to benefit.

FURTHER READING

For the student there are two ways into the field of curriculum studies, through an introductory text and through a collection of articles:

Jenkins, D. and Shipman, M. 1976. *Curriculum: an Introduction,* London, Open Books.

This introductory text is biased toward the context of the curriculum: the national and local setting to which it relates. Nevertheless, it is a readable beginning.

Kelly, A. 1977. *The Curriculum, Theory and Practice,* London, Harper and Row. Through chapters on curriculum planning, curriculum objectives, content, integration and evaluation, this introductory text raises most of the main issues in the field.

Taylor, P. and Walton, J. (Eds.), 1973. *The Curriculum: Research, Innovation and Change,* London, Ward Lock Educational.

This is a collection of papers presented at the inaugural meeting of the Standing Conference on Curriculum Studies (since transformed into the Association for the Study of the Curriculum). The papers range widely across both theoretical and practical curriculum issues.

Taylor, P. and Tye, K. (Eds.), 1975. *Curriculum, School and Society,* Windsor, NFER Publishing Co.

This text tries more deliberately than those above to provide a clear framework for the study of the curriculum by means of commentaries on selected readings.

Walton, J. (Ed.), 1971, *Curriculum Organisation and Design,* London, Ward Lock Educational.

This collection is directed largely at practical curriculum matters and contains readable articles on time-tabling, innovation and curriculum design.

For further reading on the issues raised in this chapter and in the book see references cited and summarized in *Curriculum Studies: and introductory annotated bibliography,* Richards, C., Driffield. Nafferton Books, 1978.

The following articles, all of which appear in successive issues of Volume 10, 1978, of the *Journal of Curriculum Studies,* also provide an introduction to the major issues of the curriculum field:

Shaw, K., ' Understanding the curriculum: the approach through case studies.'
Musgrove, F., ' Curriculum, culture and idealogy.'
Eisner, E., ' Humanistic trends and the curriculum field.'
Westbury, I., ' Research into classroom processes: a review of ten years' work.'

References and Notes
1. See for example *The Humanities Project: An Introduction,* 1970, London, Heinemann.
2. Plato's *The Republic* contains a classic exercise in curriculum development.
3. For instance both Rousseau and Dewey devoted much attention to education. More recently such eminent industrialists as Sir George Pickering and Sir Arnold Weinstock have aired their views.
4. This is the definition used by both INLOW, G. (1966, *The Emergent in Curriculum,* New York, Wiley.) and KERR, J. (1968, 'The problem of curriculum reform', in *Changing the Curriculum,* London, ULP.)
5. The seminal literature has been reviewed in SEGUEL, M. 1966, *The Curriculum field: its Formative Years,* New York, Teachers' College Press.
6. See STURT, M. (1967),. *The Education of the People,* London, Routledge and Kegan Paul.
7. See ASHTON, P. *et al.,* (1975), *The Aims of Primary Education: a Study of Teachers' Opinions,* London, MacMillan.
8. This point is elaborated in the Bullock Report, 1975: *A Language for Life,* London, HMSO.
9. For an elaboration of this point of view see OAKESHOTT, M. (1972). 'Education: the engagement and its frustration' in *Education and the development of reason.* Ed. Dearden, R. *et al.,* London, Routledge and Kegan Paul. 19-49.
10. PLOWDEN, B., (1967) *Children and their Primary Schools,* London HMSO.
11. See PLOWDEN, B., op. cit.
12. The *Crowther Report* (1959), *15-18,* London, HMSO gave strong support to this doctrine.
    See also TAYLOR, P. *et al.,* (1974) *The English Sixth Form,* London, Routledge and Kegan Paul.
13. A classic example is that of science. It was first advocated for inclusion in the school curriculum in the 1850's but was not generally adopted until the early part of this century.
14. See WHITMARSH, G. (1974) 'The Politics of Political Education: An Episode'. *Journal of Curriculum Studies* vol. 6, No. 2, 133-142., also the same author's M.Ed. Thesis: *Society and the School Curriculum,* University of Birmingham, Faculty of Education.
15. See FOXWELL, K. (1975). *A Comparative Analysis of Art and Craft in Four Middle Schools,* M.Ed. Dissertation, University of Birmingham, Faculty of Education.
16. See for example, WISEMAN, S., and PIDGEON, D., (1970). *Curriculum Evaluation,* Slough, NFER.
17. For an elementary introduction to the idea of systems see ACKOFF, R. and

EMERY, F., (1972). *On Purposeful Systems,* London, Tavistock Publications.
18. For contrasting approaches see BEAUCHAMP, G., (1975), *Curriculum Theory,* WILMETTE, Gagg Press, and SHAW, K., 'Negotiating Curriculum Change' in REID, W. and WALKER, D. (Eds.), (1975). *Case Studies in Curriculum Change,* London, Routledge and Kegan Paul. Also see INGLIS, F., (1974). 'Ideology and the Curriculum', *Journal of Curriculum Studies, Vol. 6, No. 1, 3-14.*
19. For an interesting essay on the relationship between scientific theory and theories concerning the achievement of desired states, see SIMON, H., (1969). *The Sciences of the Artificial,* Cambridge, Mass., MIT Press.
20. See CHEVERST, W., (1972). 'The role of the metaphor in educational thought: an essay in content analysis', *Journal of Curriculum Studies,* Vol. 4, No. 1, 71-82.

Chapter 2
Conceptions, Ideologies and the Curriculum

Introduction: *Curricula and the cultural context*

Curricula are artificial. Though to many pupils and teachers alike they have an aura of permanence and inevitability, curricula are man-made and liable to change, distortion or elaboration by those who design them and those who receive them. Social changes, political revolutions, economic transformations, advances in knowledge and re-evaluations of the past are some of the factors which serve to reshape curricula. The latter are just one of mankind's many cultural products enabling him to come to terms with the flux of events, objects, perceptions, thoughts and feelings which constitute 'the world'. Curricula, then, are not basic constituents of the natural order but are, in part at least, reflections of man's own activities and interpretations.

Curricula serve a variety of purposes, not all of which are immediately apparent. On the commonsense view they inform the young about the world in which they live. Curricula present facts about physical phenomena, they transmit scientific principles, they refer to theories and generalizations which help make sense of phenomena. In other words they describe and explain what is the case, what (in principle at least) is there in the world to observe. They also inform young people about a different range of cultural phenomena — the norms, values, conventions and classifications of their own, and sometimes other, societies. Some of these are not taught directly or explicitly, but are learnt nevertheless in the threefold interaction of teacher, pupil and curriculum. In this way curricula help transmit what human beings see as valuable, desirable, useful or convenient.

Curricula help shape the cultural experience of pupils, either by making them more consciously aware of elements previously taken for granted or by introducing them to aspects of human culture not previously encountered. Teachers are inevitably cultural agents,[1] making decisions as to what experience is desirable or valuable for their pupils. Either directly through the lessons they teach and the learning experiences they encourage or indirectly through the life of classroom and school, teachers are transmitting values. Although they may not always be conscious of it, they are daily deciding what *ought* to be taught to the young. In this way they are helping shape individual and social growth; they are both transmitting and interpreting elements of human culture.

Human culture can be looked upon as a 'stock', a body of meanings and skills used to make sense of human experience. Such a stock is unequally and differentially distributed in time, space and social structure. Thus for example, the cultural elements possessed by an English car worker are very different from those of a Samoan boat-builder, a Hittite chariot-maker or a British Leyland company director. Even within a social group as small as the family cultural components are differentiated by age and by sex. With the increasing subdivision of labour in technologically more advanced societies, more and more specialized knowledge accumulates, the total stock of knowledge increases in quantity and complexity, and the problems of selecting cultural elements for curricula increase. Through curricula teachers help transmit a sample of this ever-growing stock of meanings to the young. But a view of education as a straightforward process of information-transmission is not just over-simple but fundamentally mistaken. All sorts of problems are involved. Which parts of the expanding stock of meanings should be transmitted through curricula? Who decides this? To whom should such meanings be made available — to some or all?[2] If the former, how are the 'some' to be differentiated? How are the meanings changed during the process of transmission? How do such meanings relate to the everyday experience of the young? What constitutes successful teaching? The number of questions could be extended. The relationship between curricular decision-making and cultural elements is far more complex than a first glance suggests.

Conceptions of Education

Curricula are one means by which the young are systematically introduced to the material and non-material world they inhabit. Curricula embody perspectives from human culture considered important enough to merit systematic transmission. But unlike oral transmission of culture in technologically 'primitive' societies, curricula are found in specific institutional settings such as schools, colleges and universities. They are part of educational systems. As such they also embody beliefs about education; they invest the educational enterprise with different kinds of meaning. Embedded in them are conceptions of education — of what the enterprise is about and how it ought to be conducted. Though not always stated explicitly, and often taken-for-granted, these embedded conceptions give form to curricula, result in different curricular emphases and lead to very different practices in school and classroom. Such conceptions constitute an input into the curriculum development sub-system as indicated in Figure 3 (page 20).

No attempt is made here to spell out the multiplicity of conceptions that have shaped education in the past, but all involve the development in the young of states of mind considered desirable and characterized by knowledge and understanding.[3] However, underlying this general form are variations in views regarding what is desirable, what constitutes knowledge and understanding, and what childhood, teaching and learning are. Each of these variations will be discussed briefly to indicate how they account for the widely diverse meanings accorded education and the different curricula developed to give expression to these meanings.

(a) desirable ends
Every conception of education incorporates views of the desirable ends of the enterprise. Such views express the guiding values of those subscribing to the conception. Usually (but not always) such views are characterized in terms of particular kinds of society and particular qualities individuals need to exhibit to participate 'properly' in such societies. The ends accorded education have varied enormously in different cultural contexts: what follows simply serves to indicate this variability and some of its curricular consequences. Of necessity reference is made to those thinkers who through their writing have worked out their conceptions explicitly and who have in consequence influenced others, directly or indirectly, to hold broadly similar conceptions.

Going back over two thousand years Plato[4] conceived of

education as a means of producing a just, harmonious society and personal life. A just society was one in which the various social orders composing it were organized in a hierarchical way, the rulers ruling the state, the soldiers guarding it and the artisans providing it with economic services. In the same way in which each part of the social order kept its place and performed its proper duties, so in each individual his appetites and his passions had to be subordinated to his 'higher' nature — the rational, reflective part of his make-up. Education was to train men to fulfil their different roles in society, and different kinds of curricula were required in consequence. For example, only the rulers or guardians were to receive a thorough education in the mathematical sciences and in dialectic, since it was believed these would enable them to appreciate the eternal world of the Forms and thus govern well. Almost a thousand years later in a very different context Augustine[5] made explicit a conception of education which was to prepare pupils for obedient service in a society dominated by the Christian church. Here the desired end of education was the bringing up of the young to a love of God and to acceptance of life according to the Christian interpretation of Him. This was to be accomplished through giving pupils a general curriculum involving the seven liberal arts which revealed the divine law of both physical and social worlds and through giving a selected few studies in philosophy and theology to develop in them a rational awareness of existence, their souls and the nature of God. Thus again a differentiated curriculum was envisaged: most only studied that which was necessary for virtuous conduct and an awareness of God, whilst a few were given the opportunity to develop 'wisdom'.

More than a thousand years on from Augustine, Rousseau[6] viewed education as helping to bring about the perfectibility of man through altering his social environment. Man, he argued, was naturally good but was corrupted by his social environment. Children should be allowed to develop in their own way, so that their essential nature would be realized to the full and they would later become morally mature citizens in a society characterized by both freedom and order. This society would have a democratic form of government based on the General Will, the rational will of all society's members. Such citizens would be independent owners of property and would exhibit freedom of thought and individualism. The curriculum proposed by Rousseau was structured, orderly and disciplined with pupils' spontaneity and expressiveness contained within a carefully worked-out developmental programme. Young children were to develop through the educational exploitation of everyday life situations. Only during adolescence were they to be led into the systematic study of literature, philosophy, history, Euclidean geometry etc. In the same broad tradition as Rousseau the American philosopher, Dewey, conceived education as promoting personal 'growth' through active problem-solving in a social context. Growth for Dewey involved the extension and development of one's powers and possibilities as a human being, and for him continued growth was synonymous with successful living through the tackling and resolution of problems.[7] His proposed curricula involving children working on topics and problems which interested and challenged them reflected his concern to produce a certain type of educated man: an individual who could think for himself, make decisions, cooperate with others and participate equally as a member of a democracy.

At the present time it is in developing countries that conceptions of education are most clearly spelled out, especially when such countries are attempting to replace the vestiges of previous educational systems, now considered alien to the values of the new society. In Tanzania, for example, Nyerere has argued for the creation of a socialist society based on three principles: equality and respect for human dignity; sharing of resources; and work by everyone with exploitation by none. In pursuit of a socialist state based on a rural economy he has instituted wide-ranging reforms in the organization of schooling and in the content of the curriculum (with particular importance being given to agricultural studies). In his own words, 'We should determine the type of things taught in the schools by the things which the boy or girl ought to know — that is, the skills he ought to acquire and the values he ought to cherish if he or she is to live happily and well in a socialist and predominantly rural society, and contribute to the improvement of life there'.[8] As a further illustration, the ruling communist party of China conceive education as a means of fostering socialist consciousness and culture through developing individuals intellectually, morally and physically. Education is to unite thought and action, theory and practice, mental and physical labour, and is to play its part in three kinds of social practice — the struggle for production, the class struggle and scientific experiment. Education is to serve the ends of proletarian politics, not the pursuit of individual goals and aspirations.[9]

Current debate about English education reflects a marked lack of concensus as to the nature of the worthwhile ends of education — a point elaborated more fully later in this chapter. To illustrate, a conservative position, as exemplified by Oakeshott, conceives of education as 'the deliberate initiation of a newcomer into a human inheritance of sentiments, beliefs, imaginings, understandings and activities'[10] (p.23). The term 'inheritance' connotes the value placed on such sentiments and understandings. This transaction between generations involves the teaching of traditional academic disciplines through teacher-controlled interaction with pupils. This conception of education is countered by progressives and radicals with their own distinctive conceptions. To take one example, Holly[11] sees education as a way of liberating pupils from the domination, externalization and trivialization of traditional schooling by giving them systematic access to basic concepts and concept 'complexes' which they can employ in the determination of their own activities. In this way, he argues, education would become meaningful rather than meaningless, and school-work relevant and acceptable rather than alien. His conception of education is one of individual self-realization free from the constraints of past traditions and assumptions. Only through this kind of education, he argues, can individuals play a part in building up a genuine participatory democracy.

These then are but a sample of the many different views concerning the desirable ends of the educational enterprise. Curricula (and less directly the life of school and classroom) are the vehicles for expressing the fundamental values enshrined in such ends.

(b) knowledge
Conceptions of education also involve important ideas about the nature of knowledge. In most conceptions knowledge is assumed to be objective: a body of principles, laws, theories etc. which are external to the learner. His task is to come to terms with these public thought-forms, to understand them so that they come to inform how he views the world. Here knowledge is 'reified' — made into an object of study which exists independent of the

learner and unaffected by his own particular ways of processing data and ordering experience. Education is to initiate the learner into this knowledge, the exploration and elaboration of which constitute some of mankind's greatest achievements.

Opposed to this is a view that knowledge results from the creative power of the individual mind as it organizes experiences to form a highly complex, personal system of interpretations, intentions and recollections. Knowledge develops as, through social processes, the individual perceives logical connections between data, categorizes experience and infers increasingly complex chains of meaning. The status of knowledge as an objective entity is thus severely questioned. Knowledge is viewed as subject to individual interpretation and is in an important sense unique to every human being. The individual is seen as a 'meaning-maker' who is able to build data 'into his own scheme of things and relate it uniquely to what he already uniquely holds as experience. Thus he builds a world all his own' (p.94-95).[12]

Such relativist views find some support in the work of a group of sociologists (termed by Taylor 'the New Criticism'[13]) who argue that statements forming curricula are not statements about objective entities but are constructions put on human experience by social groups such as social classes or 'learned' professions. On this argument, though some degree of individual interpretation is inevitable, what counts as 'real' is constructed by such groups through social processes. Thus different curricula do not describe or encapsulate the same objective reality but are expressive of different realities held more or less in common by different groups in society. There are, however, cogent philosophical objections[14] to the arguments advanced for the lack of objective reality and for the total relativity of knowledge enshrined in curricula. On this view there is a material world subject to cause and effect and having distinguishable features on the basis of which communication among individuals and groups is made possible, but it is conceded that different curricula may embody different ways of looking at this world. Such stances towards the nature of knowledge are embedded in practice and thus inform the shape of curricula offered to, or negotiated with, pupils.

Another controversial issue centres on the question: 'Can knowledge be differentiated into a number of independent logical categories?' Hirst[15] argues that education is concerned with the development of pupils' knowledge and understanding, the diversity of content being determined by the diversity of logical forms that knowledge and understanding take. He distinguishes seven forms of knowledge — formal logic and mathematics, the physical sciences, moral awareness and judgment, aesthetics, philosophy, religious experience and 'our awareness of our own and other people's minds.' None of these, he claims, is ultimately reducible in character to any of the others, though inter-form connections do exist. The development of a pupil's understanding proceeds as he comes to appreciate the concepts, logical structure and truth criteria associated with each form. Other philosophers such as Phenix[16] and Broudy[17] support the general contention of the differentiated character of knowledge, though they distinguish rather different 'realms' or categories. Such analyses are often cited in support of subject divisions in curricula, though the link between a differentiated view of knowledge and a compartmentalized curriculum is not a necessary one. The assumption of differentiation is countered by those who stress the undifferentiated nature of knowledge as experienced by the individual in everyday life. Dangers are noted in the 'fragmentation' of knowledge and human experience into 'artificial compartments', dangers involved in limiting pupils' enquiries unduly, dangers in not approaching problems wholistically, dangers in preventing the emergence of an 'integrated' view of life. On this view distinctions within knowledge are primarily the result of socio/historical factors rather than inherent in the very logic of knowledge. It is believed that such distinctions should not dominate or shape curricula but only be employed if they can be seen to be relevant or useful in tackling issues and problems of significance to learners.

These different views can have important implications for the way knowledge (and thus curriculum content) is handled in schools. Bernstein[18] suggest that two major types of curricula can be distinguished: a 'collection' type where the various contents are insulated from one another by strict boundaries as in a subject-dominated timetable (in his terms an example of 'strong classification'); and an 'integrated type' where the boundaries between contents are blurred and the contents are each related to an overarching idea or concept — 'weak classification'. Along with the degree of 'framing' (see page 38) the degree of classification has important implications for the way knowledge is transmitted, the way it is viewed by learners, the identity taken by teachers and the form of social control exercised by the school.

Another set of views is concerned with the differentiation of knowledge but here in terms of inclusion in, or exclusion from, curricula. As stressed previously, all curricula involve some selection from society's stock of knowledge: all are based on the assumption that some aspects merit inclusion more than others. Attempts have been made to justify the inclusion of aspects of knowledge on a number of grounds. Peters[19], for example, argues that certain sorts of activities are presupposed when a person seriously asks the question 'Why do this rather than that?'. These activities, including science, literary appreciation and philosophy, have 'a wide-ranging cognitive content': they give endless opportunities for further study, for fresh discrimination and judgment and for further development of skills. They illuminate other aspects of life and contribute to the quality of living. Qualities such as these 'give them a value denied to other more circumscribed activities which lead us to call them serious pursuits' (p.160). Such pursuits should feature in the curricula of educational institutions. John White[20], however, provides a different justification for including some activities rather than others in compulsory curricula. He does not accept Peters' arguments summarized above. He contends that curricula should be planned so as to lead a person in the end to an awareness of the Good; that only the person himself is in a position to determine the Good for him; and that to arrive at this awareness he must know of the possible things he may want to choose for their own sake and he must be ready to consider what to choose from the point of view not only of the present moment but of his life as a whole. Compulsory curricula should comprise those activities which a person could not possibly understand without engaging in them. In this way curricula would help a person acquire sufficient understanding and awareness to enable him to choose his own version of the Good Life. Using such arguments White includes areas such as pure mathematics, physical science and art appreciation in his compulsory curriculum whilst excluding areas such as foreign languages, organized games and cookery. He does not disregard these entirely but suggests they form part of voluntary provision on offer to, but not compulsory for, young people.

In different cultural contexts different arguments are brought forward to justify the inclusion of different aspects of knowledge. For example, Soviet communist party members argue for the inclusion of the study of Marxist-Leninism since this helps shape 'socialist consciousness and the making of a communist man for a communist society'. Likewise, in Britain religious education has been defended by some as a compulsory part of the school curriculum since it is said to promote a common set of values in an age when values and standards are on the decline. The links between such arguments and beliefs about the worthwhile ends of the educational enterprise are obvious.

Recently in England there has been considerable discussion about a 'common core' curriculum, a curriculum in which certain elements would be common to all primary or secondary schools. Such elements would be identified as so fundamental and important that all pupils would be given every opportunity to acquire the skills, capabilities and understandings they generate. Developing criteria for selecting such elements, spelling out the latter and facilitating their acceptance and implementation in schools will not be easy. At present, despite frequent talk about a 'common core', it can and does signify different things to different people: for example, the same group of subjects for everyone, the same subject content for everyone, the same subject aims which might be pursued in very different ways, the same broad subject framework in which many different kinds of activities might be organized, and so on. Calls for a 'core' come from a variety of educational standpoints and arise for a number of reasons: general public disillusionment with schooling, a feeling in some quarters that state schools exhibit an unacceptable diversity of quality and opportunity, a concern on the educational 'right' for steps to achieve at least minimal 'standards', a contention from the 'left' that equality of curricular opportunity is required, if the educational system is not to discriminate more subtly than before against working-class pupils. Various aspects of knowledge have been advanced as candidates for inclusion in such a 'core'. Much remains to be done before such discussion is given curricular reality as part of the operational curriculum transacted with pupils in schools.

Some sociologists[21] argue that the more worthwhile or 'high status' aspects of the curriculum (some of which are likely to appear in diluted form in the core but offered in much greater depth for high-ability pupils) are largely reflections of the dominant power structure in society, since those in positions of power are able to define the knowledge available to them as 'educational knowledge' which they can get accepted as more worthwhile than the 'commonsense' knowledge of other groups in society. Certainly, proponents of very different conceptions of education share the basic assumption that knowledge can, and should, be differentiated according to importance or worthwhileness, but they differ among themselves as to the actual aspects accorded high-status.

(c) children and childhood

Embedded in conceptions of education and in curricula are views as to the nature of children and childhood. Such views are not often made explicit but are very influential in shaping how teachers transact curricula with children in classrooms and how they interpret children's behaviour. Two importantly different stances are taken towards the nature of childhood itself. Some conceptions (for example, those of Plato and James Mill) view childhood as merely a stage in development towards adulthood — childhood being necessarily imperfect and incomplete. Children are viewed as embryonic adults who need to be prepared for their future roles in adult society. Childhood can, however, be viewed as an end in itself; qualitatively different from adulthood but just as valuable or even more so. Here the child is to be treated as a child, an individual deserving of respect in his own right who is to be allowed to pursue his own interests without regard for his future adult roles. Though rarely taken to such extremes in practice, this assumption implies a very different form of education (and very different curricula) from the former one. Certainly it is true that schools differ considerably in the extent to which they oriente their curricula to preparing children for their future lives as adult members of society.

Two other important variations in beliefs about children's nature have influenced curricula in the past and still do to some extent. Such beliefs can be considered 'metaphysical' since they are concerned with what is believed to be the very nature of a child's being. One view, put forward by Augustine and supported by many Victorian educationists, sees children as wayward, erring, selfish —

in Calvin's terms 'the seed-bed of sin'. Adam's fall from grace in the Garden of Eden has been used to 'explain' this state of being, which in turn has been held to justify rigorous, adult-controlled training of the young. Though many teachers would not subscribe to the doctrine of 'original sin' as promulgated by Augustine or Calvin, some do believe that children are 'naturally' quarrelsome, mischievous and troublesome. A radically opposite view is that children are by nature 'good' — 'let us lay it down as an incontrovertible rule that the first impulses of nature are always right; there is no original sin in the human heart.'[22] Some kind of pattern of perfection is held to be present in embryo in each child and this reveals itself as the child develops, provided the environment (both physical and human) is appropriate. These opposing views have resulted in very different attitudes towards the way curricula should be transacted with pupils

The body/soul dichotomy is another prominent metaphysical belief which has had wide implications for the form education should take, especially its orientation towards spiritual experience. Many conceptions of education such as those with Marxist or Maoist foundations reject this dichotomy altogether whilst Plato, Augustine, Aquinas and their present-day adherents make much of it in their theories of education. To take one example, Plato conceived the soul to be superior to the body and the souls of human beings to be of differing degrees of quality, some souls having more of 'the rational' and 'the noble' than others. Selection of 'superior' human beings at an early age and consequent differentiation of curricula were justified in this way.

In addition to metaphysical beliefs there are contrasting psychological beliefs about children. On one view children are endowed with varying degrees of intellectual ability, this ability being subject to limits in every case. It manifests itself as a result of interaction between children's environment and their 'innate potential'. The latter is comprised of various factors, prominent among which is 'intelligence' that can be measured objectively through tests. Children are not assumed to be active learners but are believed to require motivation or stimulation in order to 'fulfil their potential'. Support for such a view comes from the work of Jensen[23] and from behavioural psychology which interprets human behaviour in terms of sets of stimuli and the responses they produce[24]. Taken to an extreme education is conceived by behaviourists as a mechanistic process of 'stimulus control' and behaviour shaping'. In direct contrast some educationists believe that all human beings are capable of continued intellectual development throughout childhood and adulthood and that it is false to assume the existence of limits. That children do not develop may at least in part be the result of the labels or constructions ('slow learner', 'early leaver', 'educationally subnormal') put on their behaviour by others. This view assumes a much more open notion of ability and a readiness among the young to interact with their environment. Pupils are not considered as needing motivation by external factors: they are necessarily seeking meaning and making inferences concerning the world around them. Psychological support for this viewpoint comes from workers such as Bruner[25] and Piaget[26] who stress that intellectual development is an active process in which individuals structure and organize their experience (with help from others) in progressively more complex ways. What is in dispute here are not the facts of psychological development but the meaning to be accorded such facts.

(d) teaching

Views as to what constitutes 'education' also involve beliefs as to what teaching is. As teaching is necessarily related to learning, and learning to knowledge and experience, beliefs about teaching connect with beliefs about knowledge, learning and children. Though the surface features of teaching are very varied, in fact idiosyncratic to different teachers in different classrooms, there are two major models underlying the diversity of current practice. Such models are not found in a pure form but do provide 'master patterns' orientating practice and discussion about practice in education[27].

On one view teaching in schools is a form of unequal social and intellectual interaction between representatives of different generations — between those who have status and 'worthwhile knowledge', and those who do not. Teaching is to initiate learners into valuable pre-existing knowledge forms in an orderly, systematic way. The teacher is the 'asker' of questions and the 'possessor of knowledge'; the pupil is the 'respondent' and the 'receiver'. Classroom interaction involves the teacher in didactic instruction (as the major teaching mode), in keeping 'discipline' and in promoting motivation so as to get pupils to learn. In

Bernstein's terms[28] such teaching is characterized by strong 'framing', i.e., strict control by the teacher over the selection, organization and pacing of the knowledge transmitted and received in the pupil-teacher relationship. The evaluation of such teaching and learning is through 'objective' criteria derived from knowledge forms and embodied in tests and examinations which emphasize 'right' answers and 'right' ways to these. Most conceptions of education (despite having different ends in view) and much current practice have assumed a view of teaching similar in most respects to this model. Curricula as implemented in schools have reflected it in consequence.

The second teaching model involves very different assumptions. Teaching is seen as a form of social and intellectual interaction between two equally active partners, each seeking meaning. It assumes a two-way relationship between the development of children's thinking and the teacher's structuring of knowledge — each takes account of, and works on, the other. Prominence is given, not to 'objective' knowledge structures enshrined as 'subjects' to be mastered, but to pupils' mental ordering processes. Pupils' 'commonsense knowledge' acquired outside school is not disregarded but accorded respect along with 'academic knowledge'. Didactic instruction is minimized, concept formation through active exploration on the part of pupils is stressed. Much more latitude is given in the teacher-pupil relationship. The latter is much more symmetrical: the teacher can be 'respondent' as well as 'asker', 'receiver' as well as 'possessor' — likewise the pupil. In Bernstein's terms 'framing' is weak with pupils having more say in what knowledge is transmitted and how it is transmitted in classrooms. Pupils' interests and felt concerns are paramount, thus problems of motivation are minimized. Evaluation is far less clear-cut and subject to multiple criteria, not all of them quantifiable in terms of marks or grades. This model underlies recent more 'open' approaches to teaching in the work of some primary classes and a smaller number of secondary ones.

Ideologies of Education

The previous section has illustrated some of the diversity of meanings accorded education and embodied in curricula in different contexts. These conceptions have been seen to rest on different views regarding the desirable ends of the educational enterprise and on different beliefs, often unacknowledged and implicit, about the nature of knowledge, children, teaching and learning. Conceptions are held by individuals: they have often been given particularly sharp focus in the writings of educational theorists but they underlie the practice of every individual teacher too. Although every individual's conception of education is to some degree idiosyncratic through the differing emphases placed on different elements, there is a good deal of common ground in the conceptions held by groups of individuals. Consequently it is possible to group a multiplicity of conceptions into a smaller, more manageable number of educational ideologies — systems of beliefs and values about the educational enterprise held by particular groups in societies. The ideological perspective is a useful one in helping characterize the nature of current discussion in education.

In its most general sense an ideology is a system of beliefs and values held in common by members of a social group, each of whom draws on this system of meanings in explaining the world or part of it (e.g. education). Ideologies can be religious, political, economic, even aesthetic or metaphysical, as well as educational. Ideologies contain both factual and evaluative ideas (as illustrated in previous sections) which within the ideology are taken-for-granted. Such ideas provide an explanation and justification of the group's activities. Ideologies articulate members' views of reality (or part of it), present these in a more or less coherent form and compete with other ideologies in getting their views accepted by other people in a society.

Educational ideologies represent different clusters of beliefs, values, sentiments and understandings but all purport to explain what education 'is'. They employ their own combinations of concepts and metaphors which give insight into how they view education and which give their adherents a sense of what is 'right' and 'natural' for children in schools.[29] They vary in the degree of cohesiveness and coherence of their elements and in the extent and nature of the support they receive from different sectors of intellectual opinion. They vary in the types of knowledge they consider worthwhile or of high status, in the ways they believe such knowledge should be transmitted and evaluated and in the degree to which they believe such knowledge should be made accessible to those who do not already possess it. They each have their 'gurus', their 'sacred books' and their 'texts'. To summarize, ideologies constitute systems which give meaning to the complex and diverse practical enterprise of teaching and provide general guidelines towards which this enterprise can be directed.

At this point in the discussion two warnings are in order. It would be a mistake to identify any one educational ideology exclusively with any particular social class, economic or political group in a society. An ideology may draw the bulk of its adherents from such a group, it may help serve that group's interests but many of its beliefs about education may be held by members of other groups. Again not every individual concerned with education can be identified exclusively with one ideology: frequently individuals' conceptions contain elements from more than one ideology, often in uneasy association with one another, but with one being predominant.

The interplay among ideologies in any educational system influences greatly how education is conceived by those who work in the system or by those who are its clients and consumers. On this view, what counts as 'education' is ideological in character and varies with the struggles, negotiations and compromises among groups, each with its own ideology. The English educational system provides a useful illustration of the diversity of educational ideologies, each with their distinctive views of education and curricular proposals embodying these. Davies'[30] four-fold classification of major educational idealogies ('conservative', 'revisionist', 'romantic' and 'democratic') will be adopted here. Such a classification is simple, not exhaustive (excluding for example, Marxist, existential and Catholic ideologies), yet captures more of current debate about English education than the oft-quoted 'traditional-progressive' dichotomy.

'Conservative ideology' values stability, continuity with the past and the transmission of the nation's cultural heritage. It stresses the centrality of initiating the young into this 'precious inheritance' and the necessity of an élite to preserve and extend cultural excellence. It employs concepts such as 'standards', 'high culture' 'folk culture', it uses metaphors such as 'structure', 'inheritance' and 'apprenticeship'. It takes a hierarchical, differentiated view of knowledge with some aspects such as pure mathematics, the study of literature and classics being regarded as far more worthwhile than others. It does not make such knowledge equally accessible to all but supports a differentiation of curricula for the élite and non-élite. It favours a subject-centred curriculum for the able, an emphasis on ' basic skills' in the primary school, a teacher-dominated pedagogy and a conception of 'objective knowledge' to which children have to accommodate.[31]

A 'revisionist ideology' values modernization, efficiency and the expansion of education to produce a skilled labour force. Educated manpower is regarded as one of the nation's greatest assets in international economic competition. An effective, up-dated curriculum is seen as an essential component of the nation's ability to compete. 'Vocational relevance', 'efficiency', 'evaluation' and 'renewal' are some revisionist key concepts; metaphors such as 'pools of ability', 'untapped resources' and 'wastage' are used to argue for an expanded educational system which will make the maximum use of the nation's resources. This ideology values scientific and technological studies and aims to make these available to any pupil provided he has the 'ability'. Childhood is essentially a preparation for later roles in society; children's achievements are the result of IQ plus motivation[32]; knowledge structures are objective and teaching is to be adult-managed. Such an ideology was a major thread in the 'Great Debate' of 1976-77.

'Romantic' ideology centres on the individual rather than the nation, on the present rather than the past or the future, on the child rather than the adult. It stresses the importance of the young coming to understand themselves and their environment in their own terms; it stresses spontaneity, variety of first-hand experience and diversity of response. Its key concepts include 'self-expression', 'play', 'creativity', 'active involvement', 'children's needs and interests' and 'learning by experience'[33]. It employs a rich variety of metaphors such as 'growth', 'harmony', 'discovery', and 'cultivation'. It does not recognize a hierarchy of knowledge forms and takes a subjective view of knowledge with children as constructors of their own reality. It advocates teaching as a process of mutual exploration between near-equals; it views childhood as valuable in its own right and children as seekers after their own meanings.

'Democratic socialist' ideology values equality, and supports change in education (and the wider society) in order to realize this. It stresses the importance of creating a common culture and a genuine democracy in which all social classes can participate on equal terms. Its concepts include 'equality of educational opportunity', 'relevance', 'continuing education' and 'democratic participation'. It talks of 'opening doors' to knowledge, providing 'access' to the 'high culture' for all and building on a common core of meanings. Common schools and a common curriculum feature prominently as part of its platform. Teaching is seen as open to negotiation between teacher and pupil; knowledge is objective but needs constant reinterpretation in contemporary terms. All pupils require access to these knowledge structures, though the importance of their everyday experience and 'commonsense knowledge' is also acknowledged.[34]

Such ideologies encapsulate the views of different groups, each seeking to make its particular view of education *the* view of education. The meaning accorded 'education' in any society varies according to the salience of ideologies and their ability to attract public and professional support. The relative prominence of any one ideology is not simply the result of the inherent persuasiveness of its views nor of the activities of its adherents. Ideological factors interrelate in very complex ways (which cannot be discussed adequately here) with social, technological and other cultural factors. As these factors and their interrelationships change (as they have done markedly this century) so does the salience of ideologies and views as to what and how the young ought to be taught. At a particular time such as late nineteenth century England one ideology may become dominant and impress its imprint on the pattern, organization and curricula of the educational system (or particular sectors of it). At other times (as at present in England) there may be no one dominating ideology to provide an overall sense of what education ' is'. There may only be competing definitions pulling the system in disparate directions. The result is a very varied set of curricular proposals, none of them acceptable to the vast majority of teachers and parents.

The struggle among ideologies can be viewed as a 'political' one in the sense that it influences the distribution, exercise and justification of power in society. It is a struggle for power to define education and to transmit particular beliefs and values to the young. It is power to help create reality for them; power to convey meanings, and power to withold or bestow such meanings on different children. It represents a struggle for control over the educational system, which is itself a major agency for controlling social groups. Curricula are seen, then, as not just concerned with transmitting part of the cultural stock, but as helping control people through exposing them to particular values and beliefs. Such political power exercised through the educational system and its curricula is all the more potent for being generally unrecognized in many societies. Seen from this perspective, the four ideologies in English education outlined above are as political as, for example, Soviet educational ideology which explicitly seeks 'the making of a communist man for a communist society.'[35] [36]

Curricula, then, are more than inert bodies of information: they have considerable cultural and political significance. As society changes, so proposals are put forward by individuals or groups for changes in what ought to be taught the young. Such proposals are not created from scratch but are based on understandings, beliefs and values shared by those according roughly similar meanings to 'education'. Such meanings have been the subject of this chapter and form the basic input into the curriculum system outlined on page 20. In the process of translation into more detailed proposals for intended curricula they are inevitably changed, distorted or elaborated; they are subject to constraint and compromise. Yet despite this they shape the form and direction taken by proposals for new courses of study or patterns of educational activity.

In contrast to the general nature of this chapter the next three are much more specific. They analyze in greater detail the agencies and activities by which broad conceptions and ideologies of education are given particular form in new proposals for courses of study.

Further Reading
1. Reynolds J. and Skilbeck M., *Culture and the Classroom,* London, Open Books, 1976. This book attempts to explore the relationships between culture and curriculum with particular emphasis on the cultural significance of curriculum decisions. Though uneven in quality, it has useful chapters on values, beliefs and culture, on ideology and culture and on schools and the curriculum design process. The final chapter is an interesting one where a proposal is put forward for a common core cultural curriculum.

2. Skilbeck M, *Ideologies and Values,* Unit 3, E203, Curriculum Design and Development, Milton Keynes, Open University Press, 1976. This unit provides a useful introduction to the concepts of culture, ideology and value. It discusses classical humanism, progressivism and reconstructionism as examples of educational ideologies, and it poses the question: 'What values should be embodied in the curriculum and how should they be presented to learners?'

3. Moore T., *Educational Theory: an introduction,* London, Routledge and Kegan Paul, 1974 This is a clear, non-technical examination of the nature and functions of educational theory. Its particular relevance to this chapter lies in its review and critique of the theories of Rousseau, Plato, Mill and Dewey, including the teasing out of many of their assumptions.

4. Price K., *Education and Philosophical Thought,* Boston, Allyn and Bacon, second edition, 1967. This is a fairly detailed examination of a number of philosophers and their contribution to educational theory. It provides ample illustration of the various desired ends accorded education and of some of the assumptions underlying educational theories. Philosophers featured include Plato, Augustine, Aquinas, Comenius, Kant, Herbart and Dewey.

5. Richards C. (Ed.), *Power and the Curriculum,* Driffield, Nafferton Books, 1978. This edited collection of conference papers ranges widely, discussing some of the political implications of curricula and providing a critique of those sociologists of education influenced by subjectivist, Marxist perspectives.

References and Notes
1. For development of the theme of education as cultural transmission and modification see: REYNOLDS, J. and SKILBECK, M. (1976). *Culture and the Classroom,* London, Open Books and SKILBECK, M. (1976). *Ideologies and Values,* Unit 3. E.203 Curriculum Design and Development, Milton Keynes, Open University Press.
2. For discussion of such questions see: YOUNG M. (Ed.) (1971). *Knowledge and Control,* London, Collier-Macmillan.
3. For more detailed philosophical work on the concept of education see: HIRST, P. and PETERS, R. (1970). *The Logic of Education,* London, Routledge and Kegan Paul.
4. PLATO (1955). *The Republic,* translated by H. Lee, Harmondsworth, Penguin.
5. For Augustine on education see: PRICE, K. (1967). *Education and Philosophical Thought,* Boston, Allyn and Bacon, second edition.
6. ROUSSEAU, J. (1972). Emile, London, Dent (Everyman's Library).
7. Dewey's views are summarized in : MOORE, T. (1974). *Educational Theory: an introduction,* London, Routledge and Kegan Paul.
8. NYERERE, J. (1976). 'Education for self-reliance' in *Tanzania: Education for Self-Reliance,* Case study 1, E.203, Curriculum Design and Development, Milton Keynes, Open University Press.
9. See: MAUGER, P. *et al.* (1974). *Education in China,* London, Anglo-Chinese Educational Institute.

10. OAKESHOTT, M. (1972). 'Education: the engagement and its frustration', in Dearden, R., Hirst, P. and Peters, R. (Eds.), *Education and the development of reason,* London, Routledge and Kegan Paul, 19-49.
11. HOLLY, D., (1974). *Beyond Curriculum,* London, Paladin.
12. Quoted in: POSTMAN, N. and WEINGARTNER, C. (1969). *Teaching as a subversive activity,* New York, Delacort Press, 94-95.
13. TAYLOR, W. (1978). 'Power and the Curriculum' in Richards, C. (Ed.), *Power and the Curriculum,* Driffield, Nafferton Books.
14. See: PRING, R. (1976). *Knowledge and Schooling,* London, Open Books.
15. See: HIRST, P. and PETERS, R. (1970). *op cit.*
16. PHENIX, P. (1964). *Realms of Meaning,* New York, McGraw Hill.
17. BROUDY, H. (1961). *Building a philosophy of education,* Englewood-Cliffs, Prentice-Hall.
18. BERNSTEIN, B. (1971). 'On the classification and framing of educational knowledge', in *Knowledge and Control,* Ed. Young, M. London, Collier Macmillan, 47-69.
19. PETERS, R. (1966). Ethics and Education, London, Allen and Unwin.
20. WHITE, J. (1973). *Towards a Compulsory Curriculum,* London, Routledge and Kegan Paul.
21. See: YOUNG, M. (Ed.), (1971). *Knowledge and Control,* London Collier Macmillan, chapter one.
22. See: ROUSSEAU, (1972). op cit.
23. JENSEN, A., (1969). 'How can we boost IQ and scholastic achievement?' *Harvard Educational Review,* 39, 1-123.
24. See the work of SKINNER, B.F., e.g. 'The science of learning and the art of teaching', *Harvard Educational Review,* 24, 86-97, 1954.
25. BRUNER, J. (1966). *Towards a Theory of Instruction,* Cambridge, Mass., Harvard University Press.
26. See KAMII, C. (1976). 'Pedagogical principles derived from Piaget's theory: relevance for educational practice' in Golby, M. *et al.* (Eds.) *Curriculum Design,* London, Croom Helm, 82-93.
27. This is the case even when a researcher tries to avoid such models e.g. BENNETT, S. N. (1976). *Teaching Styles and Pupil Progress,* London, Open Books.
28. BERNSTEIN, B. (1971). op cit.
29. See: CHEVERST, W. (1972). 'The role of the metaphor in educational thought: an essay in content analysis', *Journal of Curriculum Studies,* Vol. 4, No. 1, May, 1972, 71-82.
30. DAVIES, I. (1969). 'Education and social science', *New Society,* May 8. See also: HOARE, Q. (1967). 'Education: programmes or men' *New Left Review* 32.
31. For examples of 'conservative' ideology see OAKESHOTT, (1972). op cit. ELIOT, T. (1948). *Notes towards the definition of culture,* London, Faber. BANTOCK, G. (1968). *Culture, Industrialisation and Education,* London, Routledge and Kegan Paul. COX, C. and DYSON, A. (Eds.), (1969). *Black Paper Two: the Crisis in Education,* London, The Critical Quarterly Society. COX, C. and BOYSON, R. (Ed.), (1975). *Black Paper 1975,* London, Dent.
32. For a penetrating satire of such views see: YOUNG, M. (1961). *The Rise of the*

Meritocracy, Harmondsworth, Penguin.

33. For examples of ' romantic' ideology see: COOK, H. (1919). *The Play Way,* London, Heinemann. PLOWDEN, B. (1967). *Children and their Primary Schools,* London HMSO. MARSHALL, S. (1963). *An Experiment in Education,* Cambridge, Cambridge University Press.

34. For examples of 'democratic' ideology see: LAWTON, D. (1973). *Social Change, Educational Theory and Curriculum Planning,* London, ULP. WILLIAMS, R. (1965). *The Long Revolution,* Harmondsworth, Penguin. WHITE, J. (1969). 'The curriculum mongers: education in reverse', *New Society,* March.

35. See: GRANT, N. (1972). *Soviet Education,* third edition, Harmondsworth, Penguin.

36. For further discussion of the politics of curricula see: WHITTY, G. and YOUNG, M. (Eds.), (1976). *Explorations in the Politics of School Knowledge,* Driffield, Nafferton Books. YOUNG, M. and WHITTY, G. (Eds.), (1977). *Society, State and Schooling,* Lewes, Falmer Press. RICHARDS, C. (Ed.), (1978). *Power and the Curriculum,* Association for the Study of the Curriculum. Driffield, Nafferton Books.

Chapter 3
Curriculum Development

Introduction

Ideological, technological, economic and other changes in British society in the twentieth century have created considerable impetus for change in education. Changes have occurred in the meanings accorded education, in the organization and administration of the educational system, in the aims and social functions of schools, in role definitions and relationships and in the curriculum offered to, and increasingly negotiated with, pupils[1]. Comprehensive education, the community school, team-teaching, vertical grouping, 'open' classrooms, social science curricula and 'new' maths are just a sample of recent changes. There have been many more.

Of the many pressing questions facing schools in this century, 'What ought to be taught to the young in a time of change?' has become increasingly important, some would say crucial to the future of schooling as we know it. This chapter and the next two focus on curriculum development and innovation — a group of activities which have attempted to generate answers to this pressing concern. Such 'answers' as to what should be taught and learned constitute intended curricula and take many forms — syllabi, sets of work-cards, text-books, films, tapes, programmed learning materials and general guides to practice. But the creation, modification and acceptance of intended curricula are not straightforward enterprises: they are not simply technical problems of discovering clearly defined means to equally clearly defined ends. In its complexity and its interplay between fact and value, ends and means, curriculum development shares many of the concerns and problems of curriculum studies in general.

As with many concepts in education, that of 'curriculum development' is not easy to grasp and impossible to pin down definitively. It is 'elastic' with a range of meanings from one which involves almost every type of educational change to one which refers to the specific processes of planning a course of study[2].

Owen[3], for example, discusses forms of organization and instruction such as micro-teaching, team-teaching, non-streaming and vertical grouping in his examination of the management of curriculum development. Johnson[4], on the other hand, views curriculum development as the processes whereby a set of learning outcomes are derived for an educational institution, but does not see it as being concerned with how such outcomes are to be realized in the context of the classroom and the school. Both these positions seem inappropriate: one legislates too strictly the area of concern, the other renders it too loose and ill-defined.

Here a middle course has been adopted. *The term 'curriculum development' is considered as comprising those deliberately planned activities through which courses of study or patterns of educational activity are designed and presented as proposals for those in educational institutions.* Such courses intended curricula necessarily include selections from a society's stock of meanings and embody a variety of views, implicit or explicit, about purposes, knowledge, children, society, teaching and learning. The conceptions of education held by individuals participating in the development enterprise and the ideologies to which they subscribe play a crucial role in influencing how such courses are designed and presented and how they are received by teachers and pupils. No matter what ideologies are involved, curriculum development implies a degree of systematic thinking and planning in which individual decisions about content, teaching and learning are taken, not in isolation, but in relation to an overall design or framework. At one extreme curriculum development may result in curriculum innovation where radically new proposals are produced with far-reaching implications for teacher-pupil transactions. On the other hand, curriculum development may just result in the modification and reshaping of current courses of study with few new components but with a clearer articulation of the various elements comprising the course. Thus a Schools Council project team planning how musical experience can be offered younger children is engaged in curriculum development as is a mathematics department in a comprehensive school rethinking the curriculum offered sixth formers in the light of changing examination and vocational requirements. Not included under curriculum development are 'one-off' changes taken with little reflection and with no attempt to see these as part of a systematic design. Thus a teacher simply adopting a new text at the head of department's instigation, or setting up a science table in his classroom because 'everyone's doing it', or trying 'an integrated day for a day or two', is not engaged in curriculum development, though the curriculum offered children may change as a result, at least minimally and temporarily.

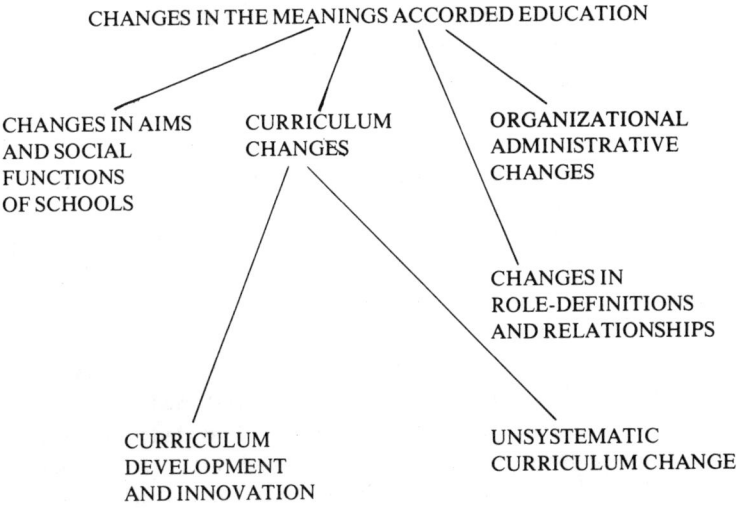

Figure 4: *Educational Change, Curriculum Change and Curriculum Development*

A digrammatic summary of the relationships among educational change, curriculum change and curriculum development is offered in Figure 4. This chapter and the next two emphasize curriculum development and innovation which result in educational proposals for use in schools, though it has to be realized that such development also applies to courses in further and higher education, especially at times when the contribution of these sectors to the educational system is under reappraisal.

Assumptions

Much has been made previously of the assumptions and beliefs underlying various conceptions and ideologies of education and informing the actions of those subscribing to them. A further set of assumptions represents those beliefs and value-judgments usually taken for granted by those engaged in the curriculum development enterprise. Rarely are these made explicit, yet the success or failure of educational proposals developed rests on their adequacy. For purposes of convenience four categories of assumptions are distinguished here: those basic to the general notion of curriculum development, those held by people professionally engaged in curriculum development, those specific to the English context and those specific to each set of curriculum proposals.

A first basic assumption is that the improvement of human experience (of which teaching and learning are facets) is both conceivable and justifiable. In other words, current conceptions of teaching, learning and curricula are not perfect or inviolable, but other conceptions can be entertained, and can be satisfactorily justified. A second basic assumption is that such improvement is possible to realise in practice, i.e. that those involved in education understand, to some extent at least, how development towards this improved state can be effected and have the freedom, ability, resources, etc., to move in the desired direction[5]. Another assumption is that changing conditions such as those brought about by socio-economic pressures or by the 'knowledge explosion' necessitate revision in what ought to be taught, the way it ought to be taught and the way it ought to be assessed. It is assumed that there ought not to be a wide cultural gap between what is learned in school and what is learned in the wider society, and between school knowledge and academic knowledge[6]. A fourth general assumption is that in the light of such changes, haphazard and uncoordinated activities on the part of individuals are not sufficient to ensure that the educational system responds to its changing social, cultural and physical environment. Individual, intuitive 'tinkering' with courses by teachers ought to be replaced by a measure of conscious planning, coordination and management at school, regional or national level to ensure that pupils receive a coherent, up-dated selection of society's developing stock of meanings.

There are a number of other assumptions specifically underlying the work of those professionally engaged full time in curriculum development. One of these is that the traditional rate of change in education is too slow and consequently needs to be accelerated by the provision of specialist agencies and structures planned on a national basis with this 'catalytic' purpose in mind. Allied to this is the notion that teachers need help and support from 'experts' if new curriculum proposals are to be developed quickly and effectively. Such 'experts' are normally subject-matter specialists but can be 'process helpers' whose expertise lies in mobilizing groups of teachers to devise their own solutions to their felt problems[7]. It has been assumed by the Schools Council and similar agencies that such expertise is in scarce supply and needs to be made available either nationally (as in a national project team)[8] or, a more recent development, locally (as consultants to groups of schools and teachers)[9]. Eraut[10] describes a further three assumptions which underlie curriculum development as practised by members of project teams. The first is that the project's strategy for getting its proposals adopted by teachers will lead to a significant number of schools implementing the educational proposals as intended (and not just employing the project's name and materials for 'cosmetic' purposes). The second assumption is that provided schools correctly implement the project's proposals, the effects on pupils, teachers and the schools will be consistent with the claims and intentions of the project team. The third is that these effects will have greater educational value than the effects of possible alternative curricular proposals.

Ways of developing curricula vary from one national context to another[11], and with each context comes a further set of assumptions about the nature of the enterprise, especially about the proper relationship among the various participants in decision-making. Bassett[12] and Richards[13] suggest some of the assumptions underlying curriculum development in the English (*not* the Scottish or Irish) context. Until very recently, and still in many quarters, it has been assumed that decisions about the curriculum are matters entirely for those professionally engaged in the education service. It is they who are to determine the appropriate response of the system to the pressures exerted on it 'from outside'. This has been an assumption shared by those subscribing to a variety of educational ideologies — 'conservative', 'revisionist' and 'romantic'. Only those subscribing to a 'democratic ideology' and those with Marxist inclinations have consistently contested this claim. A second assumption, allied to the first, is that teachers in England have a large degree of professional autonomy which enables them to determine the learning experiences they offer to pupils. Curriculum development has been seen as simply providing further options from among which teachers can choose those that they consider further the 'needs' of their own pupils. This fits in well with the further assumption that the most appropriate kind of structure with which to relate the various agencies in the educational system is a cooperative, not hierarchical, one, where persuasion rather than compulsion and guidance rather than direction are needed. At least two further major assumptions need to be made explicit. The first of these is that a significant proportion of teachers in both primary and secondary schools are agreed about the necessity for curriculum development in modifying existing courses, are willing to change their practices and have the time, energy and other resources to effect these changes. A last assumption has been that existing educational institutions, especially the notion of 'school', do not need dismantling but are fundamentally adequate to meet the challenges of the late twentieth century provided research and development are intensified, management techniques employed, communication 'improved' and 'relevant' courses developed.

These then are some of the assumptions underlying the complex of activities termed 'curriculum development'. The adequacy of these assumptions is not easy or straightforward to determine: as with the supposed autonomy of the English teacher, each may be 'a myth in the sense that it expresses great truths in a form which corresponds more to an idea than to reality.'[14] (p.10) Whatever their correspondence to reality, some at least of these assumptions are shared by a variety of agents and agencies charged with the task of devising new intended curricula in line with cultural and social changes.

Agents and Agencies
Individuals, groups, national institutions, central governments and international organizations are some of the agents and agencies who are involved in curriculum development. In no country is curriculum development the prerogative of a single institution or individual. Those actively involved in such development vary from one national context to another, since 'Who can engage in curriculum development depends in part upon how the curriculum is defined and how its function is perceived'[15] (p.10). Participants vary in the type of contribution they make, the level at which they make it, the direct or indirect nature of their contribution and the

relative freedom which they enjoy in making their contribution.

In view of the lack of detailed comparative data and of the loosely defined areas of interest and competence given to many agents and agencies, any attempt at categorizing them is bound to be imprecise. Various dimensions could form the basis of such a classification, but here two have been employed:- the salience of curriculum development among an agency's functions (and an agent's roles), and the 'arena' in which an agent or agency operates[16]. To illustrate, curriculum development could figure as the most important function of an agency or be only one among a number of concerns. The agency may operate in a national 'arena' with a national 'audience', or it may operate in a more restricted area — provincial, regional or local. An attempt is made in Figure 5 (p.54) to indicate the place of some major curriculum agencies on a grid formed from these two dimensions. The figure is not intended to be comprehensive in coverage or distribution but to indicate the range of development agents and agencies in a sample of western countries.

Figure 5. *Some major agents and agencies of curriculum development in ten countries*

	National	Provincial/regional/local
Agents and agencies with curriculum development as their major function or role	Schools Council (Eng.) S.C. project teams (Eng.) Advisory Curriculum Committees (Den.) Foundation for c.d. (Neth.) Curriculum committees (Neth.) National Pedagogic centres (Neth.) National curriculum centre (Isr.) National Consultative Ctte. on the curr. (Scot.) National c.d. centres (Scot.)	Teachers' centres (UK) Pedagogic centres (Isr.) Curr. institutes (Can.) Provincial teacher groups (Can.) Provincial institutes (Can. and W. Germany) Regional school advisory centres (Neth.) C. Development centres (USA) C. Development officers (Eng.) Directors of c. (USA) C. coordinators (UK) School advisory cttes (UK)

Agents and agencies with c.d. as one among several important concerns	Nuffield Foundation (Eng.)
	BBC, IBA (UK)
	Parliament (Den. Swed.)
	Central committees (Belg.)
	Dept. for Inservice Training (Isr.)
	Ministry of Ed. (Swed.)
	Board of Ed. (Swed.)
	University Centres
	National inspectorates*
	Publishers*
	Prof. organizations*
	  unions*
	  subject associations*
	Exam boards*
	Dept. of Ed. & Science (Eng.)
	Central Adv. Councils for Education (Eng.)
	National Foundation for Educational Research (Eng.)
		School boards (USA Neth.)
		State Ed. Departments (USA)
		Pedagogic Conferences (Belg.)
		Curr. branch of provincial administration (Can.)
		Pupils (Den.)
		Local inspectors*
		School staffs*
		Ad hoc teacher groups*
		Colleges for training teachers*
		Individual teachers*

*Where a country is not indicated after a particular agency, this indicates that such an agency is found in many of the sample countries

The countries are Belgium, Canada, Denmark, England, West Germany, the Netherlands, Israel, Scotland, Sweden and USA.

Even within the same subdivision of the grid there are many differences among agents and agencies apart from the obvious ones of staffing, funding and material provision. They vary in the independence they have from central government, in the degree of mandatory power they exercise over what is taught in schools, in the prestige they enjoy and in the length of experience and degree of expertise they bring to curriculum development. Teachers are represented to varying degrees on their managing bodies; research plays a greater or lesser part in their development work. As the volumes published by CERI demonstrate[17], some agents and agencies are concerned with the gamut of processes involved in the design, diffusion and adoption of curricula. Others are concerned mainly with one or more of the processes.

Agents and agencies in England and Wales
England and Wales provide an apt illustration of the range of institutions and interest groups involved in developing intended curricula for use in schools. At the national level the Schools Council is the only major institution specifically set up to promote curriculum development as its overriding function. It was founded in 1964 after an attempt by the Ministry of Education to take the initiative in curriculum reform through the formation of the Curriculum Study Group. Its aim has been the fostering of a 'new dynamic' in schools in the light of social and cultural changes[18]. Its policy has been spelled out in the Foreword to each of its annual reports:

> 'Its purpose is to undertake in England and Wales research and development work in curricula, teaching methods and examinations in schools, and in other ways to help teachers decide what to teach and how to teach it. In all its work it has regard to the general principle, expressed in its constitution, that each school should have the fullest possible measure of responsiblity for its own curriculum and teaching methods based on the needs of its own pupils and evolved by its own staff'[19] (p.7).'

Supporters[20] see its guiding principles as pluralism, freedom of choice for schools, involvement of teachers at all stages, partnership among sectors of the education service and the development of professional standards. With substantial annual budgets provided jointly by the Department of Education and Science and the local education authorities the Council has been a powerful influence on the development of curricula. Its main thrust has been in the sponsoring of research and development projects in all areas of the school curriculum, though it has also sponsored work on examinations and some more basic research.

Many criticisms have been levelled against it. Some overburdened teachers have regarded its efforts as too much and too soon; radical teachers have regarded them as too little and too late. The Council has been criticized for lacking a coherent, coordinated policy for curriculum development[21]; it has been attacked as an agency of the Establishment — fundamentally 'conservative' under its 'revisionist' exterior and supportive of the political and educational status-quo[22]. Young[23] suggests that it supports rather than challenges the existing stratification of knowledge and through its projects prevents a majority of the school population from participating in high-status knowledge which gives access to positions of power and influence in society. Richards[24] argues that the Council is a prisoner of its own assumptions, some of which are inadequate — especially those concerned with teacher autonomy and willingness to change established work-styles. Recently the Council's internal organization has been restructured as a result of the implementation of a review body's findings, but the Council's likely role in English education during the next decade is as yet unclear.

Another major national influence has been the Nuffield Foundation, though curriculum development has only been one of its several concerns. From 1961 onwards it funded work in a variety of areas, beginning with the sciences, branching out into mathematics and modern languages and later extending its interests into resources for learning. Its operations, 'revisionist' in character, involved the expenditure of £1.5 million and the sponsorship of over fifteen projects. The Central Advisory Councils for Education (Crowther, Newsom and Plowden) have also contributed to discussion of the curriculum by providing an overview of a particular sector, by evaluating what was taking place in relation to what was needed (see chapter 7) and by crystallizing thinking or practice already beginning to develop. They have not themselves produced radically new proposals for curriculum renewal[25]. Universities too have played a part in curriculum development, not only in providing new knowledge to be incorporated into courses of study but also in providing resources, facilities and staff for project teams. Specialist centres have also been set up to foster work in particular areas — the Centre for Science Education at Chelsea, the Language Teaching Centre at York, the Educational Technology Centre at Sussex and the Centre for Applied Research in Education at East Anglia. The

National Foundation for Educational Research has also made a contribution, through less directly, through its work on multiracial education, testing, examinations and evaluations (such as Burstall's major study of primary French[26]).

The role of central government in relation to curricular matters is certainly less strong in England than in a country such as Sweden or the USSR, but is perhaps more influential than is commonly recognized. Through its level of financing, its circulars, its policies regarding nursery education or comprehensive education, and its control over the level of school-building and the number of students entering teaching, the government has a definite, though indirect, influence on the level and direction of curriculum development. In further education, 'the forgotten sector', there has been intervention by central government in curricular questions [27] as illustrated by the spread of liberal studies following a government circular. The Department of Education and Science also promotes curriculum development through its advisory publications which survey practice and which encourage what is seen as desirable trends. *Towards the Middle School*[28] is one such example of an influential department publication. The department is also influential through its team of inspectors (HMIs) who visit all state schools, make periodic surveys and communicate information and thinking across LEA boundaries. They locate 'good practice' and inform other teachers of this, partly through periodic personal contacts and partly through a wide range of in-service courses[29]. 1976 saw the beginnings of a more positive role for the Department in curricular matters, as evidenced by the 'Great Debate' and its follow-up.

Still at a national level the contribution of examining boards is important[30]. Despite criticisms levelled against them, they have not been content simply to preserve the curriculum status-quo, but have responded positively to developments in schools. Some indeed have taken the initiative in introducing new subjects for examination (e.g. general studies, psychology, social biology), in revising existing subjects (as in the design of 'modern maths' syllabi) and in devising new methods of assessment, the most prominent being CSE and GCE Mode Three, where schools determine their own syllabus and set their own examinations, subject to the 'moderating' influence of the Boards. Subject associations too have promoted the cause of curriculum reform, especially the Association for Science Education which was closely identified with the early Nuffield Science projects, the National Association for the Teaching of English which has promoted radical rethinking about the nature of English teaching, and the two mathematical associations which have proved powerful pressure groups for the reform of mathematics teaching at both primary and secondary levels.

Finally at the national level the contribution of the media has been significant. Through their broadcasts for schools both the BBC and the IBA have made many teachers more aware of current developments and have provided practical support to encourage cautious experimentation. The BBC in particular has been very prominent in the field of in-service education through such series as 'Early Years at School' and 'Middle Years at School'. A last but very significant national agency is the commercial publisher. For a long period publishers have both reflected and pioneered new thinking and practice by publishing the work of individual teachers. In Owen's words [31] they hold ' England's longest tradition as diffusers' (p.68). Recently they have made a major contribution through their publication of Schools Council project materials and this has often involved more than simply translating ideas directly into picture and print. They are a crucially important, but much maligned and neglected, agency of curriculum development.

At a local level teachers' centres are foci of efforts at curriculum development. These first developed during the early maths and science projects sponsored by the Nuffield Foundation but later grew into a national network, supported by the Schools Council. They constitute 'a middle ground' where teachers can meet to discuss, speculate and work outside the constraints of their respective schools. 'There potential is obvious, their achievement less so'[32] (p.12). Work in such centres has been concentrated in three broad areas. Local work in support of national projects has been a prominent and successful feature of their programmes. A second focus of attention has been inservice education, where advisers, and increasingly teachers, have put on courses or run workshops. Centres have also attempted (less successfully) to promote local curriculum development. Examples of such projects include a variety of schemes for primary mathematics, work on curriculum liaison and continuity between sectors and the assembling of local resources for environmental studies. Recently, centre leaders or wardens have increasingly come to see themselves, not as dispensers of hardware or salesmen for projects, but as developers of communication networks and facilitators of the further professional development of teachers.[33] This function is also served by teams of local authority advisers. In addition to dispensing promotions and appointments, advisers see themselves as supporters of change (sometimes through giving extra resources), as experts in particular areas of the curriculum, as organizers of inservice work and as professionals able to assist schools evaluate new curricular proposals[34]. Both the Humanities Curriculum Project and Geography for the Young School Leaver illustrate the crucial role advisers can play in facilitating development. But as with teachers centres the resources, structure and standing of advisory services vary enormously according to local circumstances. Still at the local level colleges of education have played some part in diffusing information about new practices. Some have special units established by the Schools Council for this purpose; some, such as Madeley, have been instrumental in installing new projects into local schools.

At school level various agents operate. In large schools deputy heads may be given specific responsibility for the coordination and development of the curriculum; school-wide and subject-based curriculum committees may be formed; curriculum coordinators may be appointed; professional tutors may be involved in organizing programmes of staff development. At primary and middle school level, the role of 'subject' consultants is being stressed, school-based inservice education is developing, and staff meetings are being used as 'arenas' for the discussion of curriculum policy. In an increasing number of primary and secondary schools development is being seen, not as a series of discrete, 'one-off' activities, but as a continuing process which requires specific structures (and sometimes specific posts) if it is to be effectively sustained. Up to the present time parents have had little or no influence on curriculum development in schools. Over the last decade links with parents have been strengthened but on the teachers' own terms: the curriculum has remained their preserve. However there are increasing signs of parental and community disquiet: it may be that new structures will have to be found to accommodate the growing power of the local community.[35]

But mediating between all the above agents and agencies and pupils are individual teachers who have to answer directly and daily the question: 'What should be taught?' Their freedom to determine their own response is not perhaps as great as the 'myth' of teacher autonomy would suggest, the power of the local community may be growing, but the degrees of freedom allowed them in England are still considerable. Stenhouse[36] argues that teachers themselves need to be curriculum developers, monitoring their own teaching, producing proposals for change, testing out hypotheses in the classroom and drawing on the help of researchers and advisers in a cooperative process of improving teaching. Though such a view may seem utopian to many, teachers' present role as agents of curriculum development or as maintainers of the status quo cannot be gainsayed. They, along with their pupils, are the final arbiters of what goes on in schools. They determine how far conceptions of education embedded in intended curricula are realized in day-to-day teaching.

Further reading
1. CERI, *Handbook on Curriculum Development,* Paris, OECD, 1975. The handbook is a compilation of contributions of uneven quality which, taken together, provide a useful international perspective on curriculum development. The 'art' of curriculum development, its administrative and social settings, case-studies of selected projects and reflections on the nature of curriculum studies are included.

2. Taylor, P. and Johnson, M (eds.) *Curriculum Development: a comparative study,* Windsor, NFER, 1974. This is a collection of essays illustrating how curricula are developed in a sample of ten countries. The chapters examine the participants in the process, the kinds of decisions made, the way these are implemented and some of the forces impinging on the process.

3. CERI, *Case-Studies of Educational Innovation,* volumes one to four, Paris, OECD, 1973. The four volumes feature a number of detailed case-studies of how educational change (not just curriculum development) is organized and implemented in a number of countries. Volume 1 deals with central agencies and contains Nisbet's analysis of the Schools Council. Volume 2 discusses change at the regional level and includes studies of Devon and Leicestershire. Volume 3 features secondary schools and includes a study of Countesthorpe in its early days. The fourth volume summarizes and draws out implications from the first three.

Notes and References
1. See DALIN, P. (1973). *Case-studies of Educational Innovation: IV. Strategies for Innovation in Education,* Paris, OECD.
2. See TAYLOR, P. (1970). *How Teachers Plan their Courses,* Slough, NFER.
3. OWEN, J. *The Management of Curriculum Development,* Cambridge, Cambridge University Press.
4. JOHNSON, M. (1969). 'The translation of curriculum into instruction', *Journal of Curriculum Studies,* Vol. 1 No.2, 115-131.
5. For consideration of this assumption see SKILBECK, M., (1973). 'Strategies

Curriculum Development

of curriculum change', in *Equality and City Schools,* ed. Raynor, J. and Harden, J., London, RKP.

6. See RICHMOND, K. (1971). *The School Curriculum,* London, Methuen.
7. See ERAUT, M. *et al.* (1977). 'Inservice courses: their function and design: a view from providers', in *New Contexts for Teaching, Learning and Curriculum Studies,* ed. Richards, C., Horwich. Association for the Study of the Curriculum
8. See CASTON, G. (1971). 'The Schools Council in context', *Journal of Curriculum Studies,* Vol.3 No.1, 50-64.
9. An interesting example of consultancy is documented in the Ford Teaching Project, see ELLIOTT, J., and ADELMAN, C., (1975). *Ford Teaching Project,* Units 1-4, Norwich, Centre for Applied Research in Education.
10. ERAUT, M. (1976). 'Some recent evaluation studies of curriculum projects: a review', in *Curriculum Evaluation Today: Trends and Implications,* ed. Tawney, D., London, Macmillan Education.
11. For an interesting discussion of curriculum development in relation to administrative structure see CERI, (1975). *Handbook on Curriculum Development,* Paris, OECD.
12. BASSETT, G. (1970). *Innovation in Primary Education,* London, Wiley.
13. RICHARDS, C. (1974). 'The Schools Council: a critical examination', *Universities Quarterly,* Vol.28, No.3, 323-336.
14. MACLURE, J. (1968). *Curriculum Innovation in Practice,* London, HMSO.
15. TAYLOR, P., and JOHNSON, M. (eds.) (1974). *Curriculum Development: a comparative perspective,* Windsor, NFER.
16. For elaboration of the concept of 'arena' see BEAUCHAMP, G. and BEAUCHAMP, K., (1967). *Comparative Analysis of Curriculum Systems,* Wilmette, Kagg Press.
17. CERI, (1973). *Case-studies of Educational Innovation: 1. At the Central Level,* Paris, OECD.
18. Schools Council, 1965, *Change and Response,* London HMSO, iii.
19. Schools Council, 1975, *Schools Council Report 1974-75,* London, Evans/Methuen Educational.
20. See CASTON, G., op.cit.
21. For this and other criticisms see SKILBECK, M., (1975). 'School-based curriculum development and the task of inservice education' in *Inservice Education and Teachers' Centres,* ed. Adams, E., Oxford, Pergamon.
22. This view is highlighted in two articles by John White: WHITE, J., (1968). 'Instruction in obedience', *New Society,* 2-5-68, and WHITE, J., (1969). 'The curriculum mongers: education in reverse', *New Society,* 6-3-69.
23. YOUNG, M. (1972). 'The politics of educational knowledge', *Economy and Society,* Vol.1 No.2, 194-215.
24. RICHARDS, C. (1974). op.cit.
25. See KOGAN, M. and PACKWOOD, T. (1974). *Advisory Councils and Committees in Education,* London, RKP.
26. BURSTALL, C., *et al.,* (1974). *Primary French in the Balance,* Windsor, NFER.
27. See FOWLER, G. (1975). 'DES, Ministers and the curriculum', in *Curriculum Innovation* ed. Harris, A. *et. al.,* London, Croom Helm, 59-72.

28. DES, (1970). *Towards the Middle School,* London, HMSO.
29. For an interesting discussion of the functions of the inspectorate see BLACKIE, J. (1971). *Inspecting and the Inspectorate,* London, RKP.
30. As illustrated by WYATT, T. (1975). 'The GCE Examining Boards and Curriculum Development' in Harris *et al.,* op. cit., 104-114.
31. OWEN, J., op. cit.
32. CORBETT, A. (1971). *Innovation in Education-England,* Paris, OECD.
33. For a perceptive analysis of the role of teacher centre wardens see BERESFORD, C. (1974). 'Teachers' centre processes and inservice opportunities', *Cambridge Journal of Education,* Vol.4 No.2, 93-101.
34. These four functions are outlined in COLLINS, G. (1974). 'The role of the adviser in curriculum change', *Dialogue* 18, 14-16. See also BOLAM, R., *et. al.,* (1976). *The LEA Adviser and Curriculum Innovation,* University of Bristol School of Education.
35. The Taylor Report, *A New Partnership for Our Schools,* HMSO, (1977), encourages greater parental and community participation in matters concerning the curriculum.
36. STENHOUSE, L. (1975). *An Introduction to Curriculum Research and Development,* London, Heinemann.

Chapter 4
Curriculum Design

As one of their important concerns, the agents and agencies, outlined in the previous chapter, are charged with the task of helping create new courses of study or new patterns of educational activity for pupils in schools. The design of such intended curricula involves a multitude of factors — ideological, technical, epistemological, psychological, to name but some. Developing curricula in a systematic way, as opposed to piecemeal, 'one-off' modifications to current practice, is still relatively new and in consequence is both 'tentative and primitive' (p.51). [1]Three principal curriculum design models have been produced to further this enterprise. It is important to note that these three — the 'objectives', the 'process' and the 'situational' models — do not describe how curricula are in fact designed but make recommendations for design. Their recommendations or prescriptions involve differing conceptions of the teaching/planning task, and all three are in need of further refinement and elaboration. This chapter seeks to examine and evaluate these guidelines which provide frameworks through which conceptions of education can be given tangible form as curriculum proposals.

1. The 'objectives' model and its variants

This design model, greatly influenced by behavioural psychology and systematized into a coherent rationale by Tyler[2] has directed a great amount of theorizing and practical activity, especially in the United States. The Tyler rationale, as it has been called, centres on four major stages which Tyler considers essential in the development of any curriculum. The first of these involves getting clear about goals i.e. what it is hoped the curriculum will achieve. According to his view, if such goals are to be clearly formulated, vaguely-stated aims are not sufficient. Statements of goals need to indicate both the kind of behaviour to be developed in the pupil and the area of content in which the behaviour is to be applied.

Such closely formulated statements of intent are termed *objectives*. It is very important to note here that such objectives are to be specified before the remaining components of the design model are considered (i.e. objectives are to be pre-specified). In the light of such objectives the learning experiences offered children are selected at stage two. As a third stage these experiences are organized to reinforce one another and to produce a cumulative effect. The last stage is that of evaluation which examines the extent to which the objectives are realized in practice, thereby indicating in what respects the curriculum is effective and in what respects it requires modification. This basic four-stage model (Figure 6), which is cyclic in that evaluation feeds back to objectives, is often termed 'the rational planning' model on the grounds that it is rational to specify the ends of an activity before engaging in it. An alternative term sometimes used is 'means-ends' planning.

Figure 6. *The 'Tyler' Model for Curriculum Planning*

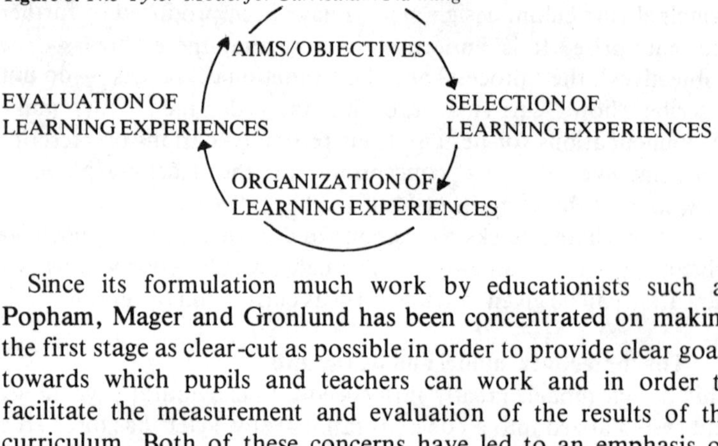

```
              AIMS/OBJECTIVES
         ↗                      ↘
EVALUATION OF                   SELECTION OF
LEARNING EXPERIENCES            LEARNING EXPERIENCES
         ↖                      ↙
              ORGANIZATION OF
              LEARNING EXPERIENCES
```

Since its formulation much work by educationists such as Popham, Mager and Gronlund has been concentrated on making the first stage as clear-cut as possible in order to provide clear goals towards which pupils and teachers can work and in order to facilitate the measurement and evaluation of the results of the curriculum. Both of these concerns have led to an emphasis on *behavioural objectives* which specify in terms of observable behaviours what a pupil should be able to do, think or feel as a result of a course of instruction. For the purpose of assessing whether or not they have been achieved such objectives have to be specific, measurable and unambiguous. Mager[3] offers an example of such an objective: 'Given a human skeleton, the student must be able to correctly identify by labelling at least forty of the following bones . . .' (p.49). A group of such psychologists[4] have produced two taxonomies to aid in the identification, description, classification and measurement of educational objectives. They distinguish three broad areas or 'domains': the *cognitive* concerned with intellectual abilities and operations, the *affective* concerned with attitudes, values and appreciations, and the *psychomotor* which covers the area of motor skills. Within the cognitive domain six broad levels of understanding (each with subdivisions) are classified, ranging from objectives concerned with simple recall of specific facts to objectives involving the evaluation of complex theories and evidence (Figure 7). Objectives in the affective domain range from those concerned with attending to phenomena to those indicating commitment to a philosophy of life. Bloom and his fellow-workers have not produced a psychomotor classification, though others have attempted to provide one[5]. By means of such classifications Bloom hopes to promote greater clarity in thinking about behavioural objectives, a more exact language for communicating about objectives and a more effective means of evaluating objectives so classified. An example of an English curriculum project considerably influenced by Bloom's approach is *Science 5-13* where initially the project director and the evaluator spent many months drawing up a list of objectives in science based on the taxonomies. Starting from an overall aim for science teaching — 'developing an enquiring mind and a scientific approach to problems' — they arrived at eight broad aims, each of which was worked out into a number of objectives, well-defined but not highly specific like Mager's. For example, under the broad aim, 'developing basic concepts and logical thinking', were objectives such as 'appreciation that things which are different may have features in common', 'formation of the notions of the horizontal and vertical' and 'appreciation of weight as a downward force'. The list of objectives tying in with stages in children's conceptual development provided a basis for curriculum evaluation and was later published to aid teachers' further thinking in this area[6].

Figure 7. *Levels in the Cognitive and Affective Domains and Sample Objectives*

A. Cognitive Domain

Level 1 **Knowledge**
'To make pupils conscious of correct form and usage in speech and writing'

'Knowledge of a relatively complete formulation of the theory of evolution'

Level 2 **Comprehension**
'Skill in translating mathematical verbal material into symbolic statements and vice versa'
'Skill in predicting continuation of trends'

Level 3 **Application**
'The ability to predict the probable effect of a change in a factor on a biological situation previously at equilibrium'

Level 4 **Analysis**
'Skill in distinguishing facts from hypotheses'

Level 5 **Synthesis**
'Ability to tell a personal experience effectively'
'Ability to propose ways of testing hypotheses'

Level 6 **Evaluation**
'The comparison of major theories, generalizations and facts about particular cultures'

B. Affective Domain

Level 1 **Receiving (attending)**
'Attends carefully when others speak in direct conversation, on the telephone, in audiences'

Level 2 **Responding**
'Finds pleasure in reading for recreation'

Level 3 **Valuing**
'Assumes responsibility for drawing reticent members of the group into conversation'

Level 4 **Organization**
'Forms judgments as to the responsibility of society for conserving human and material resources'

Level 5 **Characterization by a value or value-complex**
'Readiness to revise judgments and to change behaviour in the light of evidence'

The Tyler rationale has undergone further elaborations in an attempt to cope with the complexity and untidiness of curriculum design and its interrelations with other elements both inside and

Curriculum Design

outside educational systems. Taba[7] for example, has devoted much work to the second and third stages and has incorporated her thinking in a number of teachers' guides for elementary school social studies[8]. Goodlad and Richter[9] have tightened up the formulation of the rationale and have placed it in a wider social context by referring objectives back to educational aims and thence to a selection of society's accepted values, and by making explicit the relationship of curriculum decisions to sources of knowledge in society — 'funded knowledge' from academic disciplines and 'conventional wisdom' comprising the beliefs and understandings of members of society.

The influence of Tyler and the 'rational planning model' has not only dominated American thinking but has provided the framework for much English thinking, though less English practice. This influence is most clearly seen in a design model offered by Wheeler[10] in a book published in England in 1967. This model (Figure 8) has five basic stages, the first of these being extremely complex as general aims embodying broad conceptions of education are analyzed into ultimate goals, mediate goals, proximate goals and specific classroom objectives. These provide the direction required for the selection of learning experiences, the selection of content, the organization and integration of learning experiences and content, and the final evaluation stage which enables the designer to determine the effectiveness of the curriculum and hence to make modifications to it next time round. Its close similarity to the basic Tyler model (Figure 6) is obvious.

Figure 8. *Simple Curriculum Process Model**

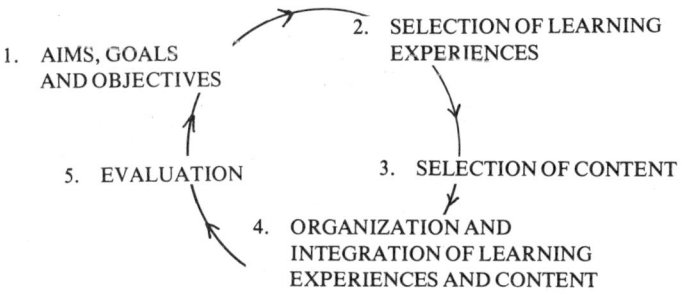

*This figure is taken from Wheeler, D., (1967). *Curriculum Process,* London, ULP, page 31.

In its stress on specific, measurable objectives at classroom level and its divorce of learning experiences and content the model is very much in the Bloomian tradition. Trace of a similar influence is found in the work of Kerr[11] who though not detailing a model for curriculum design, does offer a model of the curriculum in which objectives, knowledge, school learning experiences and evaluation feature as prominent components. His views are very much in tune with the rational planning approach e.g. 'For the purposes of curriculum design and planning it is imperative that the objectives should be identified first, as we cannot, or should not, decide 'what' or 'how' to teach in any situation until we know 'why' we are doing it. (p.21)' Perhaps the most extreme English elaboration of Tyler's basic model is Merritt's[12] eight-stage AOSTMTEC, comprising aims, objectives, strategies, tactics, methods, techniques, evaluation and consolidation. Its intricacies will not be explored here.

One last English variant should be noted. This is a suggested methodology outlined by Taylor[13] which is grounded in what a sample of secondary school teachers see as crucial factors to be taken into account in curriculum design. As such, it incorporates the prescriptions of both practitioners and a researcher in curriculum studies. It suggests beginning with the 'teaching context' — with the selection and ordering of subject-matter, the time to be devoted to teaching it and a general consideration of the methods to be employed. This is followed by a consideration of pupils' interests and attitudes which may in its turn influence the decisions already taken. Aims and objectives only appear at the third stage — 'The important thing is that objectives are integrated with full weight into this total scheme, not that they should necessarily be the starting point (p.76). Later stages include giving more specific consideration to teaching methods, justifying the course on educational grounds and trying to evaluate it in the light of the objectives stated and pupils' interests. Of the design models considered so far this places the least emphasis on objectives (though they do still feature as an important component) and appears closest to teachers' concerns through being rooted in views of practitioners actually engaged in course planning.

Rational planning models based on objectives have come in for considerable criticism.[14] They have been attacked for taking a very restricted view of rationality: 'determining ends first, then determining means' is rational in some contexts, but not always in curriculum design. Here, it is argued, ends and means cannot always be divorced; certain ends presuppose certains means and vice versa. Content and learning experiences cannot always be separated, nor can aims and content. The strictly linear treatment recommended whereby the first stage one is worked through before the second and so on is regarded as invalid: concern with one 'stage' necessarily involves simultaneous concern with other stages. Again, such models are seen as abstractions developed *'in vacuo'* circumstance inevitably arise. Another fundamental criticism of designing and planning take place and fail to appreciate the necessity for slow piecemeal change related to particular contexts and established ways and procedures. The models fail to be sensitive both to the different kinds of subject-matters which have to be planned in curricula and to the necessity for allowing flexible actions on the part of autonomous teachers as unforseen circumstances inevitably arise. A last fundamental criticism of rational planning by behavioural objectives is that within it objectives are treated as given. No adequate account is given of the source and origins of curriculum objectives in the beliefs, values and conceptions of those engaged in planning and of those influencing the planners.

Of all the components in such models, objectives (especially behavioural objectives) have attracted most criticism. No attempt is made here to summarize all the objections offered[15], but a sample of these will illustrate the lines along which objectives have been attacked. For convenience, the objections can be classified as originating in general philosophical considerations, specific discipline considerations and practical considerations. Perhaps the most telling general objection is that such important outcomes of education as understanding, appreciation and knowledge cannot be fully translated into clear-cut observable behaviours capable of measurement. Only low-level mental operations such as the recall of specific facts or the performance of certain physical skills can be unambiguously specified beforehand. The idea of translating general aims into specific objectives runs into other philosophical difficulties, where this involves specifying subsets of skills or items of knowledge (when an aim such as 'understanding the structure of our number system' is analyzed into specific components). This is far from simple and raises epistemological problems[14]. The ideal of no ambiguity is also regarded as false; objectives cannot have exact, true and real meaning, because the meaning of words depends on the way they are used, and the way they are used does vary. Objectives have also been criticized for doing violence to the nature of teaching which as an on-going activity has ends-in-view which are constantly changing, nor does the notion of prespecifying objectives before teaching take into account the autonomous nature of teacher or pupil who inevitably interpret educational processes in an individual way.[16]

Among the most vociferous critics of behavioural objectives have been those concerned with humanities, and the fine arts. Stenhouse and Eisner[17] argue very forcibly that the notion of prespecifying in advance what courses in the literary and fine arts will produce in the way of observable pupil responses does violence to the very nature of the activities engaged in. It is impossible to prespecify the nature of literary or artistic response, since such response is necessarily unique to each individual and each encounter with an art form. In aesthetic areas unpredictability and creativity are valued; prespecification results in stereotyped responses or standardized forms which do not meet aesthetic criteria; they are simply not genuine aesthetic responses or art forms. Sockett also argues[14] that prespecification violates the nature of science which rests on the assumption that everything is in principle falsifiable. As a consequence all scientific knowledge is 'provisional' in character, and not absolutely and certainly true. Prespecification presupposes that the results of scientific enquiry can be predicted with certainty, which runs counter to this basic principle and also gives pupils' a false view of the activity.

There are a number of practical objections which can also be raised against behavioural objectives. Teachers find it difficult to devise such objectives, to design curricula incorporating them and to teach with them in mind. There are problems with the tendency to over-concentrate on low-level objectives (which can be specified) to the neglect of more elusive educational outcomes which cannot be so closely delineated. Also, it is not all clear how closely objectives have to be specified in different planning situations or how they can be adequately measured using present instruments. There are difficulties too when teachers work together in planning or executing courses, since there are often differences in values and interpretation underlying superficial agreement on objectives.

In the face of such criticisms it is small wonder that advocates of rational planning by objectives have had to restate their position. Nevertheless many still support the basic approach. Hirst, for example, argues forcibly that for curriculum planning to be rational, ends have to be clarified first prior to the determination of appropriate means.[18] He agrees with many of the criticisms levelled at behavioural objectives but argues that objectives in curriculum design do not have to be expressed in behavioural terms. Such ends or objectives are very varied: they include concepts, forms of perception and judgment, patterns of aesthetic response and attitudes, which are not behaviours at all. Such 'ends can be specified in enormously varied ways, some specific, some general, some behavioural, some not.'[18] (p.141) Once objectives have been specified in appropriate detail means have to be chosen for their capacity to achieve these objectives. Both ends and means need to be justified. Hirst agrees too that such means-ends planning cannot be done *in vacuo* but must be based on a thorough understanding of the context where the curricula are to be transacted. 'What we must therefore do is to start within the context, those involved in the activity progressively making more rational what is going on.'[19] (p.14)

One of the foremost advocates of objectives-based instruction in the United States, James Popham[20], accepts that during the sixties some people were 'carried away' in their enthusiasm for clarity and measurability. He agrees that there were abuses of what he terms 'instructional objectives' e.g. too many examples of trivial behavioural objectives, too few illustrations of high-level cognitive goals or important affective goals. However, he still advocates the basic approach arguing that attempts to clarify and assess the more profound goals of education are worth making and contending that 'most educational goals can be operationalized so that we can tease out indicators of the degree to which they have been attained. Even for long-range goals we can usually find proximate predictors which, albeit less than perfect, can give us a rough fix on the degree to which the instruction is successful' (p.612).

Even two of the foremost critics of design through objectives accept that behavioural objectives have a part to play, though necessarily a limited one. Eisner[21] suggests that three broad types of objectives can usefully be employed in curriculum design, only one of which (*instructional objectives*) specifies the outcomes of a curriculum in behavioural terms. *Expressive objectives* can be used to describe learning situations intended to evoke personal responses from pupils, and *type III objectives* used to detail problematic situations, with the solutions to these problems being left to pupil initiative and justification. Stenhouse suggests that education in schools necessarily comprises at least four processes:- induction into knowledge, initiation into social norms and values, training and instruction. He argues that the objectives model is appropriate for both training and instruction but breaks down when it comes to inducting pupils into knowledge. The latter involves getting pupils on the 'inside' of knowledge forms, getting them to think creatively and to make considered judgments. According to Stenhouse, knowledge is not something to regurgitate, but something to think with. 'Education as induction into knowledge is successful to the extent that it makes the behavioural outcomes of the students unpredictable' (p.82). Improvement in education comes not from teachers being more precise about objectives but from them analyzing and criticising their own practice.

The debate about rational planning goes on: the question of the function of objectives in curriculum design is still a very open one.[22]

2. The 'process' model

This framework for curriculum design has been developed explicitly by Stenhouse,[23] though as Chapter Five indicates a variety of curricula have been developed on similar assumptions. Stenhouse argues that a process model is more appropriate than an objectives model in areas of the curriculum which centre on knowledge and understanding. Basically he contends that it is possible to design curricula rationally by specifying content and principles of procedure rather than by prespecifying the anticipated outcomes in terms of objectives. It is possible to select content on the grounds that it represents a particular form of knowledge which is intrinsically worthwhile. Content can be selected to exemplify the most important procedures, the key concepts and the criteria inherent in a form or field of knowledge. The justification for choosing such content rests not on the pupil behaviours to which it gives rise but on the degree to which it reflects the form of knowledge, which itself needs no extrinsic justification.

In areas of the curriculum such as the arts or philosophy general aims can be couched in terms of 'understanding' principles of procedure or 'appreciating' particular art forms, e.g. knowing how to conduct a philosophical argument, understanding Macbeth, appreciating a particular piece of sculpture. Planning rationally involves devising teaching methods and materials which are consistent with the principles, concepts and criteria inherent in such activities. In this design the 'process' is specified, i.e. the content being studied, the methods being employed and the criteria inherent in the activity. The end-product produced by pupils is not specified beforehand in terms of behaviours but can be evaluated after the event by the criteria built into the art form. Stenhouse illustrates how such a model can be applied to the planning of curricula in any form of knowledge: 'if you define the content of a philosophy course, define what constitutes a philosophically acceptable teaching procedure and articulate standards by which students' work is to be judged, you may be planning rationally without using objectives'[24] (p.77).

As Director of the Humanities Curriculum Project, Stenhouse has illustrated how such a design can be also used in an area of the curriculum which has no one specific form of knowledge underpinning it. This project aims at developing in pupils an understanding of social situations and human acts and the controversial value issues which they raise. It deals with themes such as *War, Poverty, Education* and *Relations between the Sexes*. It operates a discussion-based form of teaching in which the group of pupils critically examine evidence as they discuss such issues under the chairmanship of a teacher who aspires to be neutral. In the project behavioural objectives are absent: the teacher does not seek to promote any particular point of view or response in his pupils. In place of objectives the emphasis is on defining acceptable principles of procedure for dealing with such issues e.g. principles concerned with protecting divergence of opinion within the group, with developing critical standards by which evidence can be appraised, with extending the range of relevant views and perspectives accessible to the group, etc.[25]

Stenhouse's 'process model' has not as yet been subject to much criticism. It is carefully argued with reference to contemporary work in the philosophy of education. It does not seek to be all-embracing but does allow for the limited usefulness of the objectives model (p.63). It is certainly close to teachers' concerns which, as Taylor stresses (p.68), are centred around the teaching context. It does not presuppose any form of linear treatment of its components, it is sensitive to differences in subject-matter and it assumes the autonomy of the individual teacher. Hirst, however, argues[19] that the process model is still concerned with ends, though admittedly not behavioural in character, and that its emphasis on content and principles of procedure tends to obscure this necessary feature of curriculum planning. There are a number of practical objections to it, the most important being the difficulties associated with assessing pupils' work and the problems of teacher competence, since the model assumes that teachers will be refining and deepening their understanding and judgment of the concepts, principles and criteria inherent in their subjects. Stenhouse acknowledges that a process model 'is far more demanding on teachers and thus far more difficult to implement in practice, but it offers a higher degree of personal and professional development. In particular circumstances it may well prove too demanding.'[23] (p.96-7).

3. The 'situational' model

If the objectives model has its roots in behavioural psychology and the ' process' model in philosophy of education, the third major framework for design has its roots in cultural analysis. Skilbeck's[26] model locates curriculum design and development firmly within a cultural framework: it views such design as a means whereby teachers modify and transform pupil experience through providing insights into cultural values, interpretative frameworks and symbolic systems[27]. The model underlines the value-laden nature of the design process and its inevitable political character (p.42) as different pressure groups and ideological interests seek to influence the process of cultural transmission. Instead of making recommendations *in vacuo* it makes specific provision for different planning contexts by including as one of its most crucial features a critical appraisal of the school situation. The model is based on the assumption that the focus for curriculum development must be the individual school and its teachers, i.e. that school-based curriculum development is the most effective way of promoting genuine change at school-level.

The model has five major components:-

(1) *situational analysis* which involves a review of the situation and an analysis of the interacting elements constituting it. External factors to be considered

Curriculum Design

are broad social changes including ideological shifts, parental and community expectations, the changing nature of subject disciplines and the potential contribution of teacher-support systems such as colleges and universities. Internal factors include pupils and their attributes, teachers and their knowledge, skills, interests, etc., school ethos and political structure, materials, resources and felt problems.

(2) *goal formulation* with the statement of goals embracing teacher and pupil actions (though not necessarily expressed in behavioural terms). Such goals are derived from the situational analysis only in the sense that they represent decisions to modify that situation in certain respects.

(3) *programme-building* which comprises the selection of subject-matter for learning, the sequencing of teaching-learning episodes, the deployment of staff and the choice of appropriate supplementary materials and media.

(4) *interpretation and implementation* where practical problems involved in the introduction of a modified curriculum are anticipated and then hopefully overcome as the installation proceeds.

(5) *monitoring, assessment, feedback and reconstruction* which involve a much wider concept of evaluation than determining to what extent a curriculum meets its objectives. Tasks include providing on-going assessment of progress in the light of classroom experience, assessing a wide range of outcomes (including pupil attitudes and the impact on the school organization as a whole) and keeping adequate records based on responses from a variety of participants (not just pupils).

Skilbeck's 'situational' model is not an alternative to the other two: it is a more comprehensive framework which can encompass either the 'process' model or the 'objective' model depending on which aspects of the curriculum are being designed. It is flexible, adaptable and open to interpretation in the light of changing circumstances. It does not presuppose a linear progression through its components: teachers can begin at any stage and activities can develop concurrently. 'The model outlined does not presuppose a means-end analysis at all; it simple encourages teams or groups of curriculum developers to take into account different elements and aspects of the curriculum-development process, to see the process as an organic whole, and to work in a moderately systematic way'[26] (p.144). Very importantly, it forces those involved in curriculum-development to consider systematically their particular context, and it links their decisions to wider cultural and social considerations.

Support for such a 'situational' model comes from Sockett[28] who advocates a process of 'curriculum design through structure'. He sees only limited usefulness in the objectives model (mainly in the area of skills development), but does view the 'process' model as valuable. He believes that curriculum design and development have to be slow, piecemeal and uncertain, since there are a multitude of interacting factors involved and since the activities of those party to the enterprise are largely habitual. Curriculum design involves understanding the structure of the curriculum as it presently exists — or in Skilbeck's terms analyzing the situation. A first stage is to be clear about the focus of attention when anticipating change: for example, by focusing on the science curriculum of the middle school or the mathematics curriculum for the upper sixth. Then in the light of a problem (such as the possibility of introducing Nuffield Combined Science for third-year middle school pupils or individualized learning materials for A level candidates) information has to be gathered about current practices, attitudes, perceptions, influences and constraints. In this way the shape or design of the curriculum is clarified. Changes are introduced if current practices cannot be justified or if the proposed new practices are considered to offer justifiable advantages. Such changes need not be planned by objectives: they can be designed by paying attention to different aspects of the structure, to principles of procedure or to content.

Conclusion

The models outlined in this chapter are all prescriptive, recommending how the activities of curriculum design *ought* to be conducted. They constitute guiding frameworks through which beliefs, values and assumptions concerning educational purposes, subject-matter, learning and teaching are combined so as to produce intended curricula. Taken as whole the models point up the complexities of the enterprise and the varied purposes, perspectives and assumptions of writers in curriculum studies. The next chapter examines the extent to which such frameworks are followed in practice and the activities through which new courses are created, disseminated and adopted.

Further reading
1. Sockett, H., *Designing the Curriculum,* London, Open Books, London, 1976. This is a well-written introduction to the problems and possibilities of curriculum design. The author surveys the literature on design and relates his arguments closely to the school situation. He provides a critique of the objectives model, advocates a process of design through structure and puts Stenhouse's 'process' model and Skilbeck's 'situational' model in a wide perspective.

2. Tyler, R., *Basic Principles of Curriculum and instruction,* Chicago, University of

Curriculum Design

Chicago, 1949. In what is now a 'classic' text Tyler outlines his rational planning model for curriculum design. Sections deal with ways of formulating, organizing and evaluating the educational objectives that have been chosen for the curriculum.

3. Stenhouse, L., *An Introduction to Curriculum Research and Development*, London, Heinemann, 1975. Stenhouse provides an interesting but somewhat difficult textbook which attempts to define the field of curriculum studies and its problems from a personal perspective. Of particular relevance here are his chapters on behavioural objectives and curriculum development, on a critique of behavioural objectives and on the 'process' model.

Notes and References

1. STENHOUSE, L., RUDDUCK, J., and MacDONALD, B. (1971). 'Problems in curriculum research', in *Curriculum Development: an international training seminar,* ed. MacLure, J., OECD, Paris.
2. TYLER, R. (1949). *Basic Principles of Curriculum and Instruction,* Chicago, University of Chicago Press.
3. MAGER, R. (1962). *Preparing Instructional Objectives,* Palo Alto, Feanon.
4. Their work is found in:- BLOOM, B., *et. al.,* (1956). *Taxonomy of Educational Objectives: Handbook I: Cognitive Domain,* London, Longmans. KRATHWOHL, D., *et. al.,* (1964). *Taxonomy of Educational Objectives: Handbook II: Affective Domain,* London, Longmans. BLOOM, B., HASTINGS, J. and MADAUS, G., (1971). *Handbook on Formative and Summative Evaluation of Student Learning,* New York, McGraw-Hill.
5. One tentative classification is proposed by SIMPSON, E. (1966). 'The classification of educational objectives, psychomotor domain', *Illinois Journal of Home Economics,* Vol.10 110-144.
6. The published volume is ENNEVER, L., and HARLEN, W. (1972). *With Objectives in Mind,* London, MacDonald Educational.
7. TABA, H. (1962). *Curriculum Development: theory and practice,* New York, Harcourt, Brace and World.
8. TABA, H. *et. al.,* (1959). *Social Studies Grades 1-6,* Contra Costa County Schools, California. TABA, H., *et. al.,* (1971). *Teachers' Handbook for Elementary School Social Studies,* Addison Wesley, New York.
9. GOODLAD, J., and RICHTER, M. (1966). *The Development of a Conceptual System for dealing with problems of Curriculum and Instruction,* Los Angeles, University of California.
10. WHEELER, D. (1967). *Curriculum Process,* London, ULP.
11. KERR, J. (1968). 'The problem of curriculum reform', in *Changing the Curriculum,* ed. Kerr, J., London, ULP, 13-38.
12. MERRITT, J. (1972). *A framework for curriculum design,* unit 10, E283. *The Curriculum,* Bletchley, Open University Press.
13. TAYLOR, P. (1970). *How Teachers Plan their Courses,* Windsor, NFER.
14. SOCKETT, H., (1976). *Designing the Curriculum,* London, Open Books.
15. For an extensive discussion of objections to objectives see MacDONALD-ROSS, M. (1975). 'Behavioural objectives: a critical review' in *Curriculum Design,* ed. Golby, M., *et. al.,* London, Croom Helm, 355-386.

16. See PRING, R. (1973). 'Objectives and innovation: the irrelevance of theory', *London Educational Review,* Vol. 2 No.3, 46-54.
17. EISNER, E. (1967). 'Educational objectives: help or hindrance?', *School Review,* 75, 250-260 and STENHOUSE, L., (1970-71). 'Some limitations of the use of objectives in curriculum research and planning', *Paedagogica Europaea,* 73-83.
18. Taken from HIRST, P. (1973). 'Towards a logic of curriculum development', in *The Curriculum: Research, Innovation and Change,* ed. Taylor, P., and Walton, J., London, Ward Lock, 9-26.
19. HIRST, P. (1975). 'The curriculum and its objectives: a defence of piecemeal curriculum planning' in *The Curriculum,* Studies in Education 2, Windsor, NFER.
20. POPHAM, W. J. (1977). ' Objectives ' 72' ' in *Curriculum Handbook: the Disciplines, Current Movements and Instructional Methodology,* ed. Rubin, L., Boston, Allyn and Bacon, 605-613.
21. EISNER, E. (1972). 'Emerging models for educational evaluation', *School Review,* 80, 573-590.
22. For two recent interesting contributions to the objectives debate see PRATT, D. (1976). 'Humanistic goals and behavioural objectives: towards a synthesis', *Journal of Curriculum Studies,* Vol. 8 No.1, 15-26 and THOMAS, R., (1978). 'Objectives and the teaching of literature', *Journal of Curriculum Studies,* Vol. 10, No.2, 113-121.
23. STENHOUSE, L. (1975). *An Introduction to Curriculum Research and Development,* London, Heinemann.
24. STENHOUSE, L. (1970-71). *op. cit.*
25. STENHOUSE, L. (1970). *The Humanities Project: an introduction,* London, Heinemann.
26. SKILBECK, M. (1976). 'The curriculum-development process: a model for school use', in *Styles of Curriculum Development,* MacMAHON, H., unit 8, E203, Curriculum Design and Development, Milton Keynes, Open University Press.
27. For a more detailed discussion of these see REYNOLDS, J., and SKILBECK, M. (1976). *Culture and the Classroom,* London, Open Books.
28. SOCKETT, H. (1976). *op. cit.*

Chapter 5
Curriculum Change and Innovation

Development

Debate over the theoretical adequacy of design models has not prevented curricula being developed on a large scale during the last decade. This practical enterprise, though extensive in scope, has not been subject to much detailed study. The experience of different projects and schools has not been documented; the processes actually involved remain to a large extent 'curriculum mysteries'[1]. The first section of this chapter concentrates on how two major agencies have developed intended curricula. Although such curricula are generated in a variety of ways in different national contexts (see chapter three), it has been project teams and school staffs who in England have contributed most directly to answering the question 'What ought to be taught in schools?' It has been their conceptions which have found tangible form as proposed courses of study.

Curriculum Projects

Projects are investigations into specific curricular problems made over a limited period of time by teams of workers who are expressly employed for the purpose and who usually operate on a national basis. Such investigations are limited in scope, duration and material provision. By their close, they are expected to have provided at least tentative solutions to the problems outlined in their terms of reference: for example, how should history, geography and social science be taught in the middle years? or how can recent advances in physics be incorporated into a new-style A-level course? Projects are essentially 'temporary systems' existing alongside established educational institutions and attempting to catalyze them into some form of action. In England most curriculum projects have been sponsored by the Schools Council (page 55), though some local education authorities have funded local projects.

Most national projects have been based on a R.D. and D strategy, so-called because research, development and diffusion are regarded as the major stages in the development of a new pattern or product. The strategy assumes that such development is a rational enterprise, that it is planned and sequential and that the development team and their potential 'customers' share a consensus concerning objectives[2]. Two further assumptions follow. Acceptance of new ideas depends on rational persuasion, and the applicability of the solutions offered is not affected by the different contexts surrounding different users. The over-simplified, unrealistic nature of these assumptions in the complex, value-laden, partially non-rational world of education accounts for some of the problems faced by projects based on this strategy.

Although some projects such as the Aims of Primary Education project[3] have been concerned with producing research findings which increase the imformation base available to decision-makers, most projects have produced proposals for courses of study in the form of books for pupils, teacher guides, tapes, films and apparatus. How far have such projects reflected the prescriptive design models or their variants outlined in the previous chapter? When the range of projects is considered, the English picture is one of considerable diversity. Certainly it seems that many projects have not followed closely Tyler's model or its variants[4]. The early science projects financed by the Nuffield Foundation were either not concerned with, or ignorant of, objectives-based models. Many other projects such as Language in Use[5] were more concerned with producing practical suggestions for teachers than with gearing these closely to objectives. Science 5-13[6] and Nuffield A-level Biology[7] were two projects modelled on the Tyler rationale, with their aims being refined into objectives and teaching/learning strategies devised in relation to these. The North-West Regional Curriculum Project[8] also emphasized the classic four-stroke cycle of curriculum development with its panels of secondary teachers first concentrating on general and specific objectives before writing courses for early school-leavers. The History, Geography, Social Science 8-13 project was another to employ objectives, divided into skills (intellectual, social and physical) and personal qualities (interests, attitudes and values). The team originally drew these up for pupils, but later became convinced of the necessity for developing further sets of objectives for teachers, for teacher-

Curriculum Change and Innovation

educators and for themselves. Although convinced of their usefulness, the team did not take a static view of objectives, regarding their lists as provisional and subject to modification or reformulation as teachers became more fully involved in developing project ideas. In this way it was believed that objectives would not do violence to the nature of democratic curriculum development characterized by Blyth as 'awkward, largely spontaneous and never complete'[9] (p.109). Objectives have featured in other projects too but often served, at best as rather general guidelines to curriculum design, and at worst as decorative additions, peripheral rather than central to a project's concerns.

Because of its school-based rationale and its recent formulation Skilbeck's 'situational' model has not been adopted by project teams operating in a national arena, though the concern with particular contexts evinced by the Humanties Curriculum Project does come close to this. This project, already referred to on page 73, is the clearest example of the ' process' model in action. Other projects, however, illustrate Stenhouse's contention that curricula can be designed other than by the prespecification of objectives. Man, A Course of Study[10] an American social science curriculum for middle years pupils and now gaining a foothold in Britain, is designed on a specification of content and pedagogical principles. It aims to foster an understanding of the nature of man as a species and the forces that shaped and continue to shape this humanity. Major concepts such as 'life-cycle', 'structure and function', 'world-view' and 'technology' are specified as are principles of procedure for discovery/inquiry learning such as developing in pupils the process of question-posing. The curriculum does not prespecify behavioural objectives, since it is based on the belief that knowledge is provisional, speculative and thus indeterminate. Similarly, in the mid-sixties Nuffield Junior Science[11] did not specify objectives for pupils, nor did it specify content to be mastered. It was concerned instead with developing principles of procedure which would capture pupils' interests and involvement and promote their development through encouraging careful observation, recording, classification, hypothesis-formation and experimentation. Its early demise lends credence to Stenhouse's point that the process model is very demanding on teachers.

How exactly project teams have gone about designing and producing their proposals is far from clear: there are few detailed accounts of their internal operating procedures. Based on reports of American projects and first-hand investigation of the Kettering Project designed to produce curricula and instructional materials for art education in American elementary schools, Walker[12], produces a descriptive model (Figure 9) which, he argues, reflects more faithfully curriculum development as practised than do prescriptive models. According to Walker, each project member brings to the enterprise a *platform,* a system of beliefs and assumptions which guide his subsequent thinking and planning. (This is similar to an individual's conception of education referred to in chapter two). Empirical data collected by the project team and principles derived from each developer's platform are used in the *deliberation* stage when the team make decisions as a result of considering the arguments for and against alternative choices. Deliberation is also aided by a number of past decisions which constitute precedents or *policy.* As a result of such deliberation, curriculum materials are designed. The effects of design decisions can be evaluated empirically but the design itself can be justified by reference to platform principles only. Walker uses this model as a basis for understanding how the Kettering Project operated[13]. He analyzes the deliberations of the project team and concludes that the essence of curriculum development is practical reasoning where problems are identified, proposals for the resolution of these conceived and articulated, and arguments offered for and against these. There is no adherence to a step-by-step model of curriculum planning. Eisner, the director of the project, provides a complementary perspective on how the work was organized and how the team worked together.[14] He pinpoints the crucial parts played by the project's platform in providing 'an almost unarticulated convenant that gave direction to the work' and by very lengthy group deliberation as problems were presented from a variety of perspectives, and the likely effects of taking one course of action rather than another anticipated. This deliberation was akin to the deliberation of juries, where not only do facts have to be selected but values assigned to the facts. He considers that models, concepts and empirical generalizations are not 'blueprints for curriculum construction but rather mnemonic devices that enable a curriculum construction group in their more passive and reflective moments to remember what might be an important consideration' (p.38).

There are two accounts which give some indication of how English projects set about their tasks. Gray [15] describes how the English panel of the North-West Regional Curriculum Development Project operated to produce a fourth- and fifth-year course for early school leavers. He stresses the time and effort needed to reach a measure of common agreement due to the preconceptions and interpretations brought by different panel members as inputs to the development process. He charts the shifts in direction and emphasis that ensued as objectives and materials were developed. Shipman's work on the Integrated Studies

Figure 9. *A Naturalistic Model of Curriculum Development*

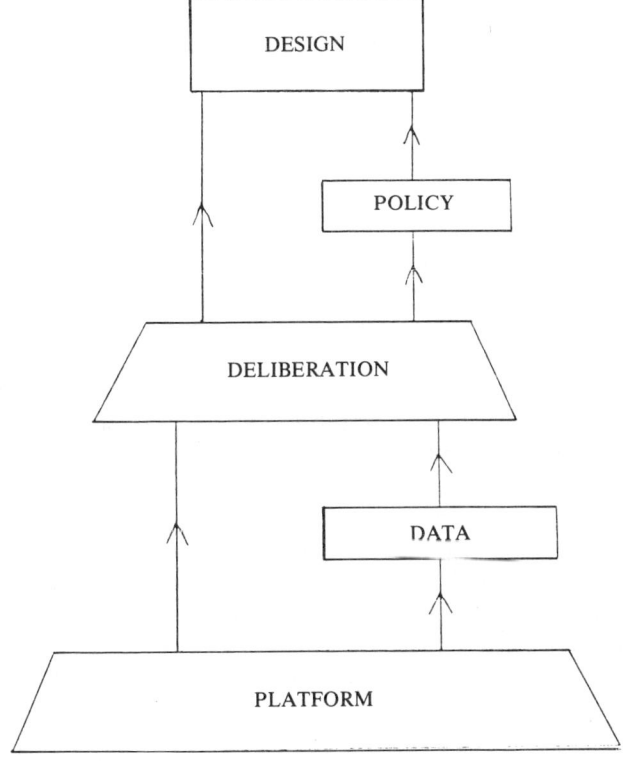

*This figure is taken from Walker, D., (1971). 'A naturalistic model for curriculum development', *School Review,* 80, page 58.

Project[16] is more concerned with the interplay among agencies in the development enterprise than with how the project team as a group interacted and negotiated with one another to produce their proposals. He does get 'inside' the project and report the different interpretations of project members towards key issues such as the nature of integration, job-definitions, division of labour and relations with others especially teachers. The book describes the pressures on the team, their uncertainty regarding procedures and outcomes and their uneasy relationships with others in the enterprise. It is clear from his account that curriculum development, at least as experienced by the Integrated Studies Project, 'does not proceed through a clear cycle from a statement of objectives to an evaluation of the learning strategies used. It is a process of bargaining, negotiation and horse-trading' (p.43).

Though Walker's model can be applied retrospectively to Shipman's account, it would be valuable to test it out fully in the English context. It would be used to examine the nature of participant's platforms, the clashes of principle, perception and interpretation which ensue, the kinds of alternative choices formulated, the decisions arrived at and the criteria for such decisions. In this way a cumulative body of knowledge regarding the internal dynamics of curriculum-building could be built-up, and future developers could benefit from others' experience.

Although the internal processes of project teams are not well documented, their external operating procedures are 'public' and have occasioned more discussion. Three main sub-strategies of the project strategy can be distinguished among English projects: those based largely on academic expertise, on teacher expertise and on teacher-project cooperation in areas where special expertise does not exist. The first project style assumes that new educational proposals are not being generated within the educational system and therefore a central team needs to be gathered together to initiate and manage the development of new courses of study. The central team creates new materials and sets up a network of trial schools in various parts of the country to test these. The centre provides the innovatory thinking; schools on the periphery respond by commenting upon the centre's proposals. Most of the 'first generation' projects, but especially the Nuffield maths and science ones, were characterized by this style[17], though many questions can be raised about its efficacy[18].

The second project style, a more recent development, works on the different assumption that new patterns of educational activity *are* being generated within the system but support needs to be given and communication improved if such patterns are to be given wider currency. Projects such as The Middle Years of Schooling Project[19] and Social Studies 8-13[20] aimed to gather information about 'good practice' and publish it in a form in which it could be used by others. This style, too, operates on a centre-periphery pattern but with the periphery playing the major part in the creation of new proposals. The centre becomes a clearing-house of periphery's ideas. Problems, however, arise as to what constitutes 'good practice' and how this can be communicated effectively to others operating in different contexts.

The third style views practising teachers as neither passive consumers of curriculum packages nor as self-generating innovators, but as partners with project teams in exploring and clarifying new approaches to teaching, usually in ill-defined areas of the curriculum. Examples of such projects include the Humanities Curriculum Project, the Integrated Studies Project and History, Geography, Social Science 8-13. Such attempts at partnership are not easy to achieve: different platforms, conflicting definitions of the situation, problems of identification, communication and over-dependence are all likely to occur. MacDonald and Rudduck[21] point up the tendency of hard-pressed teachers to become over-dependent on the central team, seeking their approval rather than testing out, criticizing and reformulating their ideas. Shipman[16] graphically documents how each group related to the Integrated Studies Project defined the situation differently and how their definitions changed as the project developed. He stresses the importance of negotiation, adaptation, and compromise if projects are to work with local agencies. He reveals an essential dilemma of the 'partnership' sub-strategy: 'Here the intention was to use grassroots initiative. But the context of contemporary teaching and curriculum development combined to frustrate this intention. Local initiatives take a lot of time, central initiatives often seem irrelevant at the local level. This is the Catch 22 of curriculum development' (p.65-66).

The 'project' has dominated curriculum development in England since the mid-sixties. Well over a hundred and fifty of these have been launched nationally and every area of the curriculum has been catered for to some extent. In developing proposals projects have encountered many problems, some of these due to their 'marginal', temporary nature — in the system, not of it. This marginal nature has never been more evident than in a time of economic stringency and retrenchment in education. The project era is fast coming to a close;[22] more attention is being focussed on small-scale curriculum development centred around the school and its problems.

Schools
Schools are specifically charged by society with planning the learning experiences of the young and immature. Schools receive help in this from the agencies discussed in chapter three, but it is in schools that the question 'What should be taught?' has to be faced directly, and proposals made, adapted or adopted in relation to it. Schools produce many proposals for courses of study:- schemes of work, concept check-lists, plans, programmes, prospectuses, syllabuses. But little is known about how these originate, the principles employed in their production, the methodologies used, the interpersonal processes involved and the ideological clashes that ensue.

Knowledge of how teachers plan intended curricula is scanty, but what evidence there is points to an expedient, short-term response to immediate problems rather than considered reappraisal of objectives and learning experiences in the light of changing circumstances. No research has been published into how primary school teachers plan their curricula, though Jackson[23] does indicate how, in the American context at least, classroom decisions are characterized by spontaneity, immediacy and irrationality rather than by reasoned consideration of objectives. He suggests that such attributes may have considerable value in allowing teachers to cope with the unpredictable, uncertain and often chaotic world of the elementary school classroom, but he does suggest a place for rational, systematic planning in what he calls the period of 'preactive teaching' before the children enter the classroom. Though prescriptive rather than descriptive Ashton's[24] work based on detailed discussions with primary school teachers indicates how aims can be translated into practice through a step-by-step planning strategy.[11]

At the secondary level Taylor[25] has examined how English, geography and science teachers proceeded with planning. As a result of analyses based on discussions, syllabuses and questionnaires, he characterizes such planning as 'rather unsystematic' and incomplete. Much of the teachers' planning seemed to be intuitive, governed by rule-of-thumb and drawing on past experience. It was a far cry from the 'logical' sequence of the 'rational planning model' or the considered thinking recommended by advocates of the 'process' model. In their actual planning the secondary teachers gave greatest prominence to pupils' needs, interests and abilities; subject-matter and aims were not regarded as so important; teaching methods were less prominent too and 'evaluation emerges as the concept in planning which teachers seem least to value or implement' (p.51). Bates[26] confirms the *ad hoc* approach in many schools. After visiting fifty comprehensive schools he admits that 'few schools have come up with a good method for planning the curriculum' (p.447) and argues that the procedures used rarely took account of the requirements of all the parties involved — parents, pupils, staff and the school itself considered as an entity. As a result he puts forward his own prescriptive model of the administrative processes involved in planning. At a micro-level Richardson[27] provides an interesting glimpse of some of the inter-personal complexities involved in planning courses in a large comprehensive school. Her account sensitises readers to the negotiations and compromises involved in such processes, but her research itself concentrates on the management of the school and does not analyze curriculum planning in any detail. Thus despite its widespread nature the planning and production of school curricula is still a 'mystery', or if not a 'mystery' at least 'a shared secret'.

Even though there is a lack of detailed knowledge concerning planning procedures in schools, a shift in emphasis at policy level can be detected away from project-based development towards school-based curriculum development. The 'centre-periphery' pattern of the R.D. and D. strategy is giving ground to what Havelock[28] terms a 'problem-solving' strategy. Here schools initiate the process of change by identifying areas of concern or sensing the need for change. They translate these needs into definable problems and then devise solutions to these either through their own efforts alone or through recruiting the help of 'outside experts'. Unlike the R.D. and D. strategy which assumes a passive consumer, the 'problem-solving' strategy involves schools in actively solving their own problems. The stress is on local initiative and local commitment to reform, with project teams, advisers college staff and others viewed as potential 'consultants' and with project materials seen as resources to be 'mined' rather than packages to be applied. Skilbeck's ' situational' model (page 74) provides a design framework which can be used as part of this overall strategy. Stenhouse[29] provides further support, arguing that with the help of educationalists in a consultancy role, teachers can be encouraged to research into their own problems and test their hypotheses in the classroom situation. In this way their professional skills can be refined, their understanding of teaching deepened and a contribution made to the beliefs that 'ideas should encounter the discipline of practice and that practice should be principled by ideas' (p.3).

A number of examples illustrate the 'problem-solving' approach in action. Eraut[30] provides a brief case-study of Granville Comprehensive School where in response to the need to provide a measure of continuity with feeder primary schools, a first year integrated humanities course was devised as a result of cooperative planning by several subject departments supported by consultation with local inspectors, heads of local primary schools, LEA architects and Institute of Education staff. Evans and Groarke[31] provide a detailed account of how a primary school staff developed and installed programmes of language development for younger children. A twelve stage 'procedural model' was drawn up by the two principal 'change-agents' and implemented carefully and sensitively, with scope for participation and comment from the remaining staff at every stage. Outside agencies were not involved directly, though relevant educational literature was drawn on heavily and support and interest elicited from the chief education officer. The authors conclude that participation in such a school-based exercise is the best medium for the inservice education of teachers. Elliott and Adelman[32] in the Ford Teaching Project provided a consultancy role for groups of teachers in East Anglia anxious to implement more effectively discovery/enquiry approaches in their classrooms. The two consultants helped teachers to clarify their thinking in this area, analyzed four different patterns of informal teaching, and through observing teachers in action, discussing teaching performances with teachers and pupils and encouraging the former to monitor their own teaching, they devised and tested a number of generalizations concerning teaching strategies. The move towards school-based development, with or without consultancy help, is growing. The experience of schools such as Nailsea, Stantonbury and Countesthorpe operating along these lines should provide valuable pointers to possibilities and problems.

This trend is part of a larger international trend towards participatory decision-making, with those affected by planning decisions becoming increasingly involved in such decisions. At school-level this calls for new planning skills, new managerial skills — what Taylor[33] terms 'procedural' and 'political' leadership. Teacher involvement in the process of curriculum development and in collegial decision-making offers an opportunity to enhance the professionalism of teachers, but makes heavy demands in return, demands which some may not wish to discharge. Not only is there the problem of managing conflict among staff, but parents, pupils and the local community are likely to become increasingly involved, with the promise of further clashes in perceptions, values and expectations. The cultural, social and ideological implications of the school curriculum will be highlighted.

INTENDED CURRICULA - the products of curriculum development

Many intended curricula have been developed since 1960. New courses, new learning materials, new teaching approaches and new forms of organization have been devised for use in schools. No attempt can be made here to describe this variety in any detail. At a national level the Schools Council's projects cover all areas of the curriculum and cater to some extent for all age-groups.[34] The Council is now engaged in plugging small gaps in its coverage, though certain sectors such as nursery and special education have not received as much attention as others. At a more local level curriculum development is also taking place, though this is not so carefully documented. For example, many secondary schools are experimenting with CSE Mode III courses, many are devising common core curricula for at least the first three years of secondary school, many primary schools are rethinking their curricula in the light of Bullock[35] and Bennett[36], many middle schools are reviewing their curricula following an initial period of experimentation. Many study groups have been set up in teachers' centres and have produced discussion documents on matters of curriculum, teaching methods, assessment and organization. Certainly in all types of school there seems a greater awareness among teachers of viable alternatives to current practice and a willingness among *some* to make changes deliberately and systematically.

Curriculum development can be profound or slight in its implications for practice. Radical curriculum innovation is a rare phenomenon, though perhaps the Humanities Curriculum Project comes closest to this characterization. The project team have pioneered an almost completely new approach to the study of controversial social problems by secondary school pupils. As indicated in Chapter Four, this approach centres on class discussion of reference material with the teacher cast in the role of neutral chairman whose concern is that each pupil should come to his own decision on rational grounds. The team have produced a very carefully worked out teaching strategy and have produced sets of reference material for pupils including reproductions of articles, extracts from books, pictures, tapes and films, all used to back up themes such as 'Poverty', 'War' or 'Relations' between the sexes'. No other project has been quite so innovatory with respect to content and pedagogy.

With the introduction of technological studies into the secondary school curriculum, Project Technology[37] represents another curriculum innovation, though its innovatory impact is largely confined to creating a favourable educational climate for such studies than with producing materials or developing methods. It has however pioneered some multi-media courses within the general field of technology and has produced enrichment materials to enable teachers to add a technological strand to their work. In the primary field no one project or innovation parallel to the Humanities Curriculum Project can be cited, but the introduction of primary French and the development of the initial teaching alphabet (i.t.a.) as a medium for teaching early reading are innovative, at least in terms of content. In general it is doubtful whether the majority of both primary and secondary projects can be regarded as radically innovative, since they tend to grow out of, and modify, pre-existing practices. Most propose moderate changes in content and teaching methods. More up-to-date material, greater use of educational technology and apparatus, and a greater stress on pupil initiative and activity characterize many of them. Thus the Nuffield 'O' and 'A' level courses in physics, biology and chemistry have developed out of, rather than revolutionized, practice in schools. The Integrated Studies Project has built on past experience of secondary school humanities teaching and has attempted an integrative, team-teaching approach. Likewise most local efforts at curriculum development are modifications, rather than radical innovations; many are little more than more careful systematizations of current practice.

Every project has produced teachers' materials whether in the form of detailed teachers' handbooks or more general guidelines. Many produce some pupils' materials in the form of texts, workbooks, assignment cards, tapes and other reference material. Increasingly, projects are producing inservice materials, as for example the tape-slide sequences produced by the Art and Craft Education 8-13 Project[38] for use in teachers' centres and colleges of education. Induction courses are prominent features of project activity such as those run by the Humanities team in East Anglia. Other projects have set up on-going teacher groups to promote their ideas in local areas; this has been a prominent feature in the strategy adopted by History, Geography, Social Science 8-13. Products of local development work are not so available nor so well-known, but new syllabi, schemes of work, 'cottage industry' resources and course outlines are becoming increasingly common in schools and teachers' centres.

Proposals for courses of study have proliferated during the last decade. Developing materials and proposals is not easy, but getting them known to, and accepted by, those in schools is a complex matter.

Diffusion and Dissemination

Once developed, a new or modified course may be implemented by the person producing it without any attempt on his part to inform or influence his colleagues. In most cases, however, information about such an intended curriculum does spread from its point of origin. It may only be to a neighbouring classroom or to members of the same department, but it can spread much further afield. In particular, curriculum projects have tried to influence the decisions of teachers on a national scale through giving them information about the nature of their proposals. 'Diffusion' is the general term used to refer to the ways in which information about curricula spreads through educational systems. 'Dissemination' can usefully be thought of as a term pointing up those diffusion processes which involve systematically planned attempts at providing information so that individuals can understand what new curricula involve.

In examining how information about curricula is diffused or disseminated models have been borrowed from other areas of study, in particular rural sociology and management theory. One such framework is the 'social interaction' model,[39] used by sociologists studying the diffusion of agricultural innovations[40]. With this perspective educational systems are viewed as complex networks of social relations along which information is passed, with some institutions and individuals being central to the network, some more peripheral and some almost isolated. New practices develop in different parts of educational systems and news about them is transmitted through the networks. In the process the 'message' is invariably altered by the preconceptions, interests and perspectives of those doing the transmitting. How quickly an individual receives information about a new proposal and how 'pure' the information is depends on the person's position in the network relative to the source of proposal. Working within this 'social interaction' framework House[41] relates it to an urban context and suggests that here the pattern of spread changes. Whereas in rural areas communication spreads in regular waves from sources of change through personal face-to-face contacts, in urbanised areas new proposals leap from one large concentration of population to the next largest in size. Unlike in rural areas, size is more important than distance in determining the rate of spread.

Schon[42] outlines three other dissemination models, each expressly concerned with the management of information concerning new patterns or products. In his 'centre-periphery' model the process of dissemination is managed centrally with proposals being fully developed and 'tooled up' prior to their dispatch from the centre to users on the periphery. A variant of this, 'the proliferation of centres' model, involves a differentiation into primary and secondary centres with the former supporting the latter in their task of more local dissemination. Schon's third model is a learning system's network in which there is no permanent centre or semi-permanent set of definitive proposals but instead a continuously changing set of ideas, a number of shifting centres and a highly developed communications system which connects all parts of the network.

There are a number of factors which are influential in determining the effectiveness of dissemination strategies based on such models. One important element is the input of energy and resources not only at the point of initiation of new curricula but throughout the system. In particular, the level of local authority support is very crucial and is determined by factors such as the size of the authority, its financing and staffing policies, the number of its advisory personnel, the way they perceive their role, and the influence of individual personalities. The nature of the communication links formed, whether personal (courses, conferences, informal contacts) or formal (mass media, books, journals) are important as are the strengths of such links and their direction (one-way, or two-way thus enabling feedback to take place). This was pinpointed by Rudduck's[43] study of the dissemination of the Humanities Curriculum Project which stresses the crucial importance of both a communication structure and of a systematic programme of training and support. The nature of the proposals being diffused also affects dissemination: it is likely, for example, that proposals enshrined in teaching/learning materials for pupils are more effectively diffused than new educational principles not embodied in the form of such materials. Rudduck argues that the dissemination of the Humanities Project is conditioned by its nature — it is complex (especially some of its concepts such as 'procedural neutrality'), it is controversial, it has no existing curriculum base and it is demanding in terms of human and material resources. All these factors make it that much more difficult to disseminate. Kelly[44] also suggests that the form of a communication — its quantity, timing, style, orientation and level — affect the quality and rate of dissemination. Further research will probably isolate further crucial factors.

Three of the four dissemination models can be usefully employed in examining English practice. The 'social interaction' model mirrors the way in which new ideas have been diffused for most of this century. In England new practices were, and still are to a large extent, spread through social networks, with HMIs, local advisors, courses and informal contacts being important elements. The 'centre-periphery' model captures the essential features of the dissemination strategy adopted by publishers where materials are produced centrally in a final form prior to sales campaigns to get these into schools. The Schools Council has tended to operate a 'proliferation of centres' model. The primary centres are the Council itself, institutions such as the Centre for Applied Research in Education or project members seconded temporarily for a period of 'after-care'. Secondary centres are teachers' centres, development centres, newly established regional dissemination centres and sometimes individual schools (where these have been involved as trial schools in individual projects). The primary centre provides written information, promotes conferences and may also run courses where it trains leaders who are to operate in secondary centres with local teacher groups.

Ungoed-Thomas[45] suggest that three phases can be distinguished in the relations between curriculum projects and dissemination activities. In early projects dissemination procedures were not built in: it was considered that the quality of the materials produced would be sufficient to ensure widespread diffusion and adoption of new proposals. Later projects had a dissemination phase following the development phase but the former was not organically related to evaluation, research or trials. Resources and time were allocated specifically for setting up an information network and network of local groups to act as diffusers once the project teams had disbanded. Recently the notion of dissemination as a separate stage has been questioned. Dissemination is being seen as 'dynamic, developing and gaining in significance from the initial phase of the project through the period beyond publication, when it will become perhaps the most significant element of the project's concerns' (p.63).

There has not been much research into dissemination in England. One important piece of work is Rudduck's sensitively-portrayed case-study of the Humanities Curriculum Project.[43] She describes the features that have made dissemination difficult and the consequent need for a strategy involving the training of people who offer local support, communication and training to teachers willing to experiment with the approach. Open days, central training courses, the formation of regional associations, the establishment of a communications network, the development of inservice materials and liaison with local education authoritives have been some of the components of the dissemination strategy. Problems of communication, authority support and training have been highlighted as has the very varied nature of LEA reponse. She concludes 'There was — and should be — no master plan for the dissemination of a project'. This view is supported by the Curriculum Diffusion Research Project[46] which investigated the diffusion of science projects by means of questionnaires, data from examining boards and case-studies of particular projects. According to this research, authorities and schools rarely use organized strategies for dissemination, temporary groups (such as groups of interested local teachers) and unofficial leadership play important roles, but overall the pattern is very diverse. 'Unique patterns of factors perceived in a variety of forms and linked to unique patterns of communicating and decision-making have contributed to a variety of responses to the advent of curriculum development projects' (p.22).[46]

A good deal of time, energy and resources have been devoted (rather belatedly perhaps) to dissemination in England, but the major problem in curriculum reform is not primarily one of communication so that informed choices can be made. The major task is to get those in schools to consider and adopt proposals for change, whether these are imported from 'outside' or developed within the institution.

ADOPTION (including implementation)

However well organized, dissemination of information does not guarantee that proposals for intended curricula will be acceptable to, and accepted by, individual schools and teachers. Adoption involves more than understanding what is communicated about a curriculum proposal. To adopt a proposal implies at least an acceptance of it as a guide to practice, but such acceptance can be token in the sense that it does not result in any changes of practice at classroom level. It is possible to speak of adoption in a fuller sense, where the proposal is not only accepted 'in principle' but is implemented (with modifications) in particular school contexts. Here, adoption is used in this fuller sense and thus includes acceptance, implementation and adaptation.[47]

Because of the inadequacies of dissemination and the difficulties of ensuring adoption of new proposals, school-based curriculum development is being proposed as a way of gaining the cooperation and involvement of teachers in the task of reshaping courses. But for some time to come at least, most proposals for new curricula are likely to originate outside any particular school, and strategies are required if these proposals are to be considered and accepted, even if acceptance leads to drastic adaptation in the light of local circumstances.

Chin[48] identifies three main types of strategy employed in fostering planned organizational change. His distinctions are useful in describing three different strategies used to promote the adoption of curricula. Each of these is 'rooted in a particular image of the practitioner'[49]. 'Empirical-rational' strategies assume that potential adopters are reasonable and will act in a rational way. The main task of the agent or agency promoting change is to demonstrate clearly the superiority and greater effectiveness of the new proposals compared with those they are to replace. These strategies underlie most attempts at promoting curriculum change in the recent past: teacher guides, pamphlets, publicity materials and conferences are all measures employed to foster the intellectual acceptance of new curricula. 'Power-coercive' strategies assume that potential adopters are powerless functionaries who are to be forced to comply with the plans, directions and leadership of those with greater administrative or political power. Since the withdrawal of the Revised Code, such strategies have not been employed on a national scale in England, though doubtless individual headteachers or heads of department have tried to foster adoption of their proposals by such means. Such forms of administrative/political intervention do characterize adoption of curricula in educational systems such as that of the USSR and other East European states. 'Normative-reeducative' strategies assume that would-be adopters are in principle willing to cooperate provided they can appreciate the relevance of new proposals to the problems facing them. What is important is how they see their problems. The strategies involve not just supplying appropriate information but changing attitudes, skills, values and relationships so that problems are seen in a new light. Change-agents work with potential adopters in interactive situations; group dynamics are employed to foster attitudes conducive to acceptance. This strategy underlies some inservice workshops mounted in England such as those concerned with new approaches to primary mathematics; it is an important feature of the concept of school-based curriculum development discussed earlier.

Many factors influence adoption but the central importance of personal factors needs to be stressed. 'Every teacher invests a considerable part of his career in acquiring a set of loyalties, professional commitments and intellectual perspectives . . . the adoption of innovatory principles and subsequent commitment to them require substantial transformation of an individual's identity.[50] (p.107). New curricula and even substantial modifications of current practice threaten teachers' established identities and the values and attitudes which sustain them. They require changes in work-styles[33] and relationships which may well threaten the fragile basis of classroom control. Such changes also impose an additional burden, that of initial incompetence. In MacDonald's words[51], 'Genuine innovation begets incompetence. It deskills teacher and pupil alike, suppressing acquired competences and demanding the development of new ones . . . In the end the discomfort will be resolved one way or the other, by reversion to previous practice or by achieving new skills and new frameworks' (p.91-2).

The institutional context constitutes another set of factors affecting adoption decisions. The stability of an institution, its leadership, its formal structure, its patterns of communication and decision-making and the roles taken by its teachers all play a part in influencing an awareness of possible changes, a willingness to examine existing practice critically and a capacity to adopt (and adapt) new proposals in a way which endures their effectiveness. According to MacMullen[52] autocratic and bureaucratic organizations are likely to stifle creative responses to problems. Organizations operating along consultative lines are likely to generate incremental change by being open to pressure from various interest groups but are unlikely to gain the whole-hearted support of junior staff and pupils. Collegiate decision-making may result in greater involvement of all the staff but may prove resistant to change from without. Participatory decision-making by both staff and pupils is likely to generate incremental change, to be resistant to fundamental changes in academic matters, but may accept far reaching changes in social relationships.

The nature of the proposals themselves radically affects their chances of adoption or adaptation. They may be variations on current practice, easily assimilable without disruption; they may involve more substantial alterations but keep the current overall framework intact; or they may necessitate radical restructuring and reorganization. Rogers and Shoemaker[53] isolate a number of other properties likely to make proposals more or less acceptable: their ease of explanation and communication to others (communicability), possibility of trial on a partial and limited basis (divisibility), difficulty of use (complexity), congruence with existing values and patterns of behaviour (compatibility), and intrinsic superiority over what already exists (relative advantage). All these properties may be important, irrespective of the actual content embodied in new curricula.

The amount of research undertaken on adoption of curricula has not been great. American research on innovation in a variety of fields[53] indicates that the pattern of adoption follows a predictable S-shaped curve with a very slow rate to begin with, followed by a period of rapid adoption and concluding with another long period characterized by a slow rate of adoption. Mort and his colleagues[54] have related adoption with levels of financial provision in school districts and conclude that it is a very slow process: they cite a period of fifteen years before a new proposal is accepted by 3 per cent of schools. Their empirical work was undertaken over a decade ago and their pessimistic conclusions may now be invalid because of more recent attempts at the management of dissemination and adoption. A recent large-scale study by Mann and others[55] has investigated the impact of four federal programmes (Right to Read, Vocational Education, Bilingual Education and a variety of Title III activities) aimed at promoting educational change in American schools by funding innovative projects for a trial period. From their survey of 293 projects and their closer examination of 29, they stress the importance for adoption of mutual adaptation by projects and schools and of the creation of receptive institutional settings. They conclude:

'The main factors affecting innovations were the institutional setting, particularly organizational climate and the motivations of participants, the implementation strategy employed by local innovators to install the project treatment, and the scope of change implied by the project relative to its setting. Neither the technology nor the project resources nor the different federal management strategies influenced outcomes in major ways. Thus project outcomes did not depend primarily on 'inputs' from outside but on internal factors and local decisions' (p.23 volume IV).

Within a 'social interaction' framework Carlson[56] relates the adoption of certain developments such as modern maths and team-teaching to the social characteristics of superintendents of school systems. Early adopting systems have superintendents who have a high social involvement with other superintendents and who also have high social status. In a second study[57] he documents some of the unanticipated consequences of the introduction of programmed instruction. He suggests that this threatened the relations between teachers and principals because the former were no longer responsible for the content of instruction and their performance could not be judged on traditional criteria. As a consequence instead of encouraging individual rates of progress as intended, they confined the variations in pupil progress. They reinstituted some 'normal' teaching to satisfy their need to 'perform' and their need for security. Corwin[58] analyses the relationship between a large number of variables and the degree of innovativeness of schools. He suggests that the most important facilitating factors are a well educated, experienced staff, moral support for change from the local community, resources for change available from outside schools, schools large enough to provide some additional resources, and communities large enough to offer pressure points for change. Much the same findings emerge from Yegge's[59] work on the adoption of Harvard Project Physics. Most of the American research has been questionnaire-based, though Smith and Keith[60] and Gross, Giacquinta and Bernstein[61] provide case-studies of unsuccessful innovation in two American elementary schools. Both studies illustrate the uncertainty among teachers as to what the proposed changes involved and both highlight the extreme difficulty of changing established work-styles.

In England information about adoption is scanty. The Curriculum Diffusion Research Project reports that the rate of uptake of Nuffield O level projects has followed the predicted S-shaped curve so that by 1972 6 per cent of possible candidates were being entered for new-style O-level biology, 15 per cent for chemistry and $12\frac{1}{2}$ per cent for physics. A survey carried out by HMIs in 1973 indicated that 30 per cent of eligible schools were 'doing' Nuffield Combined Science, 20 per cent Nuffield A level chemistry and smaller percentages other projects, though far larger numbers of schools claimed to be using the materials in part. MacDonald and Walker[62] claim that a third of all secondary schools had adopted Geography for the Young School Leaver within fifteen months of its materials being commercially available. Other measures of interest in new curricula are available: the number of candidates for new-style GCE and CSE mode III examinations, the purchase of materials from publishers, the readership of Schools Council Working papers[63] and the volume of enquiries at the Council's information centre. Such figures are encouraging to proponents of change: they do show that many schools and teachers are aware of new developments and want to know more about them. But they are only indications. Purchasing materials does not mean they will be used appropriately; buying a working paper does not necessarily result in any new work being done; entering pupils for a 'new' examination does not guarantee that they have been taught using 'new' methods.

English research into adoption has been small so information is not available to 'flesh out' these indications. One major national research project, 'Success and Failure and Recent Innovation', has spent a considerable period of time investigating how a sample of secondary school projects have been received in schools. The results of its case-study approach have not been fully reported at the time of writing. It was not until 1976 that the Schools Council finally commissioned a project to monitor the uptake of its materials.[64] In May 1978 this Impact and Take-Up Project published a first interim report based on a survey of primary schools. Its findings suggest that there has been some use made of Schools Council and Nuffield projects but not on an extensive scale. In particular, 80-85 per cent of primary heads claim that at least one project is being 'used' in their schools. However, on similar evidence, over half the projects examined are being 'used' in less than 10 per cent of schools. Other research has been small-scale. Smith[65] relates the adoption of Nuffield Junior Science to the activities of a small group of activists who were engaged in the project from its early stages and attempted to sustain momentum after the initial phase. The long-term adoption of the project's approach was hindered by the migration of these activists. Bennett's[66] survey of teaching 'styles' in the North-West of England suggests that the adoption of child-centred styles has been far less widespread than commonly supposed. Brown's[67] survey of fifteen primary schools known to have adopted at least one of three innovations stresses the importance of the head in making adoption decisions and the almost casual approach to curriculum development in the schools. The crucial role of the head is also illusttated by Dickinson's[68] study of middle schools in Hull and Shipman's account of trial schools in the Integrated Studies Project. Other small-scale studies are reported in a survey by Harding, Kelly and Nicodemus[69] written as part of their work on the Curriculum Diffusion Project.

Although conclusive objective evidence is lacking, there is a widespread feeling among educationists that adoption strategies have not been all that successful and that the first decade of curriculum development in England has had only a major effect on a minority of schools, even if it has affected many more in minor ways. Hoyle, for example, suggests that the R.D. and D. strategy 'has been less successful than some protagonists hoped'[70] (p.13). MacDonald and Rudduck[21] describe a phenomenon they term 'innovation without change'. Blyth[71] talks of the 'failure of previous projects to make a lasting impact' (p.47). Rudd[72] describes progress with school-based innovation as 'disappointingly slow' (p.54). However, before a judgment is made regarding the degree to which schools have accepted new proposals, the warning of MacDonald and Walker needs to be heeded.[62] They suggest that project teams engage in 'image manipulation' — presenting one image to teachers and a different one to their academic colleagues and critics. What teachers implement may well be very close to the image the project team put over, though this may be very different from the image held by educationists. Thus what is appropriate implementation from one perspective may seem like failure to adopt proposals in a pure form from another.

Whatever the degree of adoption, there is no doubt that some progress at least has been made in curriculum development in the last decade. Its complexities and imponderables are being exposed, a language for discussing curriculum change is being developed, a bank of valuable teaching/learning materials is being produced and expertise in the development of resources is accumulating. A foundation is being laid for future curriculum development even though this may take a very different form from the project-dominated work of the late-sixties.

Conclusion

The question 'What ought to be taught to the young?' has always been important — to society itself, to its various constituent groups and to the young themselves. It has been asked in the past but it has not always generated an imaginative, forceful response in the form of carefully considered practical proposals for intended curricula. During the last decade or so the question has been asked more urgently and a more systematic response has been made to it. Curriculum development is more than an educational or pedagogic response: it has political, ideological, social and economic implications, as it helps shape the young's view of themselves and their world. Because of its concern with what ought to be taught and with what education 'means' it cannot be value-free. It is inevitably a focus for value-conflicts and its management is both 'a practical and political art'[73]. This art is equally important at the next stage of curriculum process where proposals for intended curricula are transacted and carried out in practical terms by teachers and pupils.

Because of its mixture of fact and value, actuality and possibility, art and science, the study of curriculum development is best approached through a variety of perspectives. These demonstrate its untidiness, its imperfections and its complexities, but they are beginning to provide a measure of order and coherence to this important sphere of educational activity. In doing this, they are unlikely to remove entirely the particular, the personal, the intricacy and the inconsistency inherent in such a complex, value-saturated activity — it is these that provide much of the fascination, and frustration, of curriculum studies and curriculum development.

Further Reading

1. Schools Council, *Pattern and Variation in Curriculum Development Projects,* London, Macmillan Education 1973. This is a clearly written account of the various patterns of development adopted by sixteen English curriculum development projects. It explores why projects were set up, their aims, products and ways of working. The final chapter provides a number of interesting issues for consideration.

2. SHIPMAN, M., (1974). *Inside a Curriculum Project,* London, Methuen. This is an interesting account of how the Keele Integrated Studies Project originated, developed and altered. It charts the differences in perception among those involved and it throws light on the relationships among project teams, local authorities, heads and class teachers.

3. TAYLOR, P.,(1970).*How Teachers Plan their Courses.* Windsor, NFER. This is a research report which traces the planning procedures adopted by a sample of secondary school teachers of geography, science and English. In his last chapter the author puts forward a model for curriculum planning based on his research.

4. REID, W., and WALKER, D., (eds.), (1975). *Case-Studies of Educational Change,* London, RKP. The book features six detailed case-studies drawn from the United States and the United Kingdom. Walker's article, 'Curriculum development in an art project' is particularly interesting, as are the contributions by Hamilton and Dickinson.

5. HOYLE, E., (1976). *Strategies of Curriculum Change,* Unit 23, E203, Curriculum Design and Development, Milton Keynes, Open University Press. This is a useful introduction to some of the concepts employed in discussions of curriculum change. It also summarizes the main features of strategies for organizational and curriculum change, along with their advantages and disadvantages.

6. PRESCOTT, W., (1976) *School-based Curriculum Development,* Unit 26, Curriculum Design and Development, Milton Keynes, Open University Press. This explores the strengths and weaknesses of the arguments in favour of school-based curriculum development. Three themes are emphasized: the role of the school and the teacher; the need for participation in decision-making and the need for effective supporting agencies.

7. BECHER, T., and MacLURE, S., (1978). *The Politics of Curriculum Change,* London, Hutchinson. This is a well-written, thought-provoking analysis of curriculum development since 1945. It introduces a number of new concepts which help make sense of the complexities of development activities.

References and Notes
1. See BECHER, T. (1973). 'Curriculum mysteries', *Times Educational Supplement,* 26-10-73.
2. See DALIN, P. (1973). *Case Studies of Educational Innovation: IV. Strategies for Innovation in Education,* Paris, OECD.
3. ASHTON, P. *et al.,* (1975). *The Aims of Primary Education: a Study of Teachers' Opinions,* London, Macmillan Education
4. For a very useful survey of early projects see Schools Council, 1973, *Pattern and Variation in Curriculum Development Projects,* London, Macmillan Education.
5. The Language in Use materials were published by E.J. Arnold, from 1971.
6. The materials from the Science 5-13 project are published by MacDonald Educational. For an overview of the project's strategy see ENNEVER, L., and HARLEN, W., (1972). *With Objectives in Mind,* London, MacDonald Educational and HARLEN, W. (1975). *Science 5-13: a Formative Evaluation,* London, Macmillan Education.
7. Materials in Nuffield Advanced Level Biological Science series were published by Penguin Education, 1970-71.

8. The North-West Regional Curriculum Development Project materials were published by Blackie and Holmes McDougall. For a view of the project see RUDD, W., (1968). 'The North-West Regional Curriculum Development Project' *Forum,* 10, 40-42.
9. BLYTH, W. (1974). 'One development project's awkward thinking about objectives', *Journal of Curriculum Studies,* Vol. 6, No.2, 99-111.
10. The course materials for MACOS were produced by Education Development Centre, Cambridge, Massachusetts and are available in Britain from the Centre for Applied Research in Education, University of East Anglia.
11. The Nuffield Junior Science Teacher Guides were published by Collins in 1967.
12. WALKER, D. (1971). 'A naturalistic model for curriculum development', *School Review,* 80, 51-65.
13. WALKER, D. (1975). 'Curriculum Development in an Art Project', in *Case Studies in Curriculum Change: Great Britain and the United States,* REID, W. and Walker, D., (eds.), London, Routledge and Kegan Paul, 91-135.
14. EISNER, E. (1975). 'Curriculum Development in Stanford University's Kettering Project: Recollections and Ruminations', *Journal of Curriculum Studies,* Vol. 7, No.1, 26-41.
15. GRAY, K. (1974). 'What can teachers contribute to curriculum development?' *Journal of Curriculum Studies,* Vol. 6, No.2, 120-132.
16. SHIPMAN, M. (1974). *Inside a Curriculum Project: a case-study in the process of curriculum change,* London, Methuen. Shipman's account also contains a perceptive account of the relations between the project team and the trial teachers: JENKINS, D., ' Schools, teachers and curriculum change', 94-120.
17. For an account of 'first-generation' project development see BANKS, L. (1969). 'Curriculum Developments in Britain 1963-68', *Journal of Curriculum Studies,* Vol. 1, No.3, 247-259.
18. See HOYLE, E., (1973). 'Strategies of curriculum change', in *In Service Training: structure and content,* (ed.), Watkins, R., London, Ward Lock, The two reports produced by the project are BADCOCK, E. *et. al.,* (1972). examination', *Universities Quarterly,* Vol. 28, No.3, 323-336.
19. The two reports produced by the project are BADCOCK, E. *et. al.* (1972). *Education in the Middle Years,* London, Evans/Methuen Educational. ROSS, A., *et. al.,* (1975). *The Curriculum in the Middle Years,* London, Evans/Methuen Educational.
20. See LAWTON, D. *et. al.,*(1971). *Social Studies 8-13,* London, Evans/Methuen Educational.
21. MacDONALD, B. and RUDDUCK, J. (1971). 'Curriculum research and development projects: barriers to success', *British Journal of Educational Psychology,* 41, 148-154.
22. For an interesting analysis see MacDONALD, B. and WALKER, R. (1976). *Changing the Curriculum,* London, Open Books.
23. JACKSON, P. (1968). *Life in Classrooms,* New York, Holt, Rinehart and Winston.
24. ASHTON, P. *et. al.,* (1975). *Aims into Practice in the Primary School,* London, ULP.
25. TAYLOR, P., (1970). *How Teachers Plan their Courses,* Windsor, NFER.

26. BATES, A. (1973). ' The planning of the curriculum', in FOWLER, G. *et. al.*, *Decision-Making in British Education*, London, Heinemann, 446-461.
27. RICHARDSON, E. (1973). *The Teacher, The School and The Task of Management*, London, Heinemann.
28. HAVELOCK, R. (1971). 'The utilization of educational research and development', *British Journal of Educational Technology*, Vol. 2, No.2, 84-98.
29. STENHOUSE, L. (1975). *An Introduction to Curriculum Research and development*, London Heinemann.
30. ERAUT, M. (1972). *Inservice Education for Innovation*, London, NECT.
31. EVANS, P. and GROARKE, M. (1975). 'An exercise in managing curriculum development in a primary school' in *Aims Influence and Change in the Primary School Curriculum*, Taylor, P., (ed.), Windsor, NFER, 103-137.
32. See ELLIOTT, J. and ADELMAN, C. (1975). *Ford Teaching Project*, Units 1-4, Norwich, Centre for Applied Research in Education.
33. TAYLOR, P. (1977). 'Educational innovation: the politics and the processes' in *New Contexts for Teaching, Learning, and Curriculum Studies*, Richards, C. (ed.), Horwich, Association for the Study of the Curriculum.
34. Schools Council (1976). *Project Profiles*, London, Schools Council Information Centre.
35. BULLOCK, A. *et. al.*, (1975). *A Language for Life*, London, HMSO.
36. BENNETT, N., *et. al.*, (1976). *Teaching Styles and Pupil Progress*, London, Open Books.
37. Project Technology materials are published by Heinemann Educational, English Universities Press, E. J. Arnold, Blackie and Son and University of London Press.
38. The Art and Craft Education 8-13 Project materials are published by Van Nostrand Reinhold.
39. The term is Havelock's *op. cit.*
40. As illustrated by the work of Rogers. See ROGERS, E. (1962). *Diffusion of Innovations*, New York, Free Press, and ROGERS, E. and SHOEMAKER, F. (1971). *Communication of Innovations*, New York, Free Press.
41. HOUSE, E. (1974). *The Politics of Educational Innovation*, Berkeley, McCutchan.
42. SCHON, D. (1971). *Beyond the Stable State*, London, Temple Smith.
43. RUDDUCK, J. (1976). *Dissemination of Innovation: the Humanities Curriculum Project*, London, Evans/Methuen.
44. KELLY, P. (1970-71). ' The process of curriculum innovation' in *Paedagogica Europaea*, 84-106.
45. UNGOED-THOMAS, J. (1974). 'Dissemination, process and training', *Cambridge Journal of Education*, Vol. 4, No.2, 60-64.
46. For findings of the Curriculum Diffusion Research Project see HARDING, J., KELLY, P. and NICODEMUS, R. (1976). 'The study of curriculum change', *Studies in Science Education*, Vol. 3.
47. For a discussion of the concepts for adoption, dissemination and implementation see ELLIOTT, J. (1977). *Dissemination and related concepts*, PLS Dissemination Study, Schools Council Publications.
48. CHIN, R. (1968). 'Basic strategies and procedures in effecting change' in

Designing Education for the Future, Morphet, E. and Ryan, C. (eds.), New York, Citation.

49. SIEBER, S. (1972). 'Images of the practitioner and strategies of educational change', *Sociology of Education,* 362-385.
50. ESLAND, G. (1972). ' Innovation in the School', Unit 12, *School and Society,* E282, Bletchley, Open University Press.
51. MacDONALD, B. (1973). 'Innovation and Incompetence', in *Towards Judgment,* HAMINGSON, D. (ed.), Norwich, Centre for Applied Research in Education, Occasional Publications No.1, 89-92.
52. McMULLEN, T. (1973). 'Organization and relationships within the school' in *Creativity of the School,* Paris, OECD, 62-83.
53. See ROGERS, E. and SHOEMAKER, F. (1971). op. cit.
54. MORT, P. (1964). 'Studies in educational innovation from the Institute of Administration, an overview' in *Innovation in Education,* Miles, M., (ed.), New York, Teachers College Press.
55. Rand Corporation (1975). *Federal Programs Supporting Educational Change,* volumes I-V, Santa Monica, Rand Corporation.
56. CARLSON, R. (1965). *Adoption of Educational Innovations,* Eugene, University of Oregon, Centre for the Advanced Study of Educational Administration.
57. CARLSON, (1965). op. cit.
58. CORWIN, R. (1975). 'Innovation in organizations: the case of schools', *Sociology of Education,* 48, 1-37.
59. YEGGE, J. *et. al.,* (1971). 'The decision-making process in the adoption of a new physics course in American high schools', final report, United States National Science Foundation.
60. SMITH, L. and KEITH, P. (1971). *Anatomy of Educational Innovation,* New York, Wiley.
61. GROSS, N. *et. al.,* (1971). *Implementing Organizational Innovations,* New York, Harper Row.
62. MacDONALD and WALKER (1976). op. cit.
63. See Department of Education and Science, (1970). *Survey of Inservice Training for Teachers 1967,* Statistics of Education S52, London, HMSO.
64. STEADMAN, S., PARSONS, C. and SALTER, B. (1978). *Impact and Take-Up Project: a First Interim Report to the Programme Committee of the Schools Council,* London, Schools Councils Publications.
65. SMITH, M. (1971). 'Curriculum change at the local level', *Journal of Curriculum Studies,* Vol. 3, No.2, 158-162.
66. BENNETT, N. *et. al.,* (1976). op. cit.
67. BROWN, M. (1971). 'Some strategies used in primary schools for initiating and implementing change', unpublished M.Ed. thesis, University of Manchester.
68. DICKINSON, N. (1975). 'The head teacher as innovator: a study of an English school district', in *Case Studies in Curriculum Change: Great Britain and the United States,* Reid, W., and Walker, D., (eds.), London, Routledge and Kegan Paul.
69. HARDING, KELLY and NICODEMUS, op. cit.
70. HOYLE, (1973). op. cit.

71. BLYTH, W. (1973). ' History, Geography and Social Science 8-13 — a second-generation project', in Taylor, P., and Walton, J., (eds.), *The Curriculum,* London, Ward Lock, 40-51.
72. RUDD, W. (1973). 'Teachers as curriculum developers: a second-generation viewpoint' in *The Curriculum,* Taylor, P., and Walton, J., (eds.), London, Ward Lock, 52-64.
73. STENHOUSE, L. (1973). 'A matter of style', *Times Educational Supplement,* 27.4.73

Chapter 6
The Curriculum in Operation and in Context

Introduction
As already noted, a curriculum, whether developed anew or remaining virtually unchanged over the years, embodies educational intentions — knowledge to be understood, skills to be learned and attitudes and values to be acquired. For these intentions to be realized teaching and learning have to take place — the intended curriculum resulting from curriculum development has to be operationalized. The way in which teaching is done, the psychological conditions under which learning takes place, together with the social and institutional setting in which they are enacted, influence what curricular intentions are achieved. Different teaching-learning 'milieux' affect the meaning acquired by pupils from their curricular experience. This chapter seeks to understand how educational intentions are achieved by exploring the curriculum in operation and in context.

Time and its allocation
Of the many factors influencing the modifications, compromises and accommodations which accompany the translation of intended into operational curricula, time and its allocation are of crucial importance. Time is a major influence on the shape of operational curricula in all schools, whether it is an 'open' primary school with an integrated day or a tightly time-tabled comprehensive school catering for both examination and non-examination pupils. This is the least elastic factor with which the operational curriculum has to make an accommodation: there is only so much of it in the school day, week and year. How to use it for curricular purposes is a decision which in most schools involves the head, usually in

consultation with the staff, and is one which indicates the value placed on particular curricular activities. The valuation is not always put into practical application as the work of Davies[1] has suggested: rather it roughly accords with the educational purposes to be served[2]. Decisions about time may be merely routine:- to carry out the allocations of time that have been made previously. If so, such decisions confirm previously accepted valuations about what is to be taught.

There are two basic ways in which curricular time may be allocated: (a) in units of lessons or periods, some of which may be doubled or blocked as whole mornings or afternoons, and (b) wholistically, as in the 'integrated day' in the primary school, where time is spent much more flexibly by individuals or small groups (and occasionally the whole class) on learning within broad subject areas or from purposefully designed educational activities and materials. Whichever way curricular time is used, the amount of time spent on a subject or an educational activity tends to represent a valuation of that subject or activity. The relationship between time and value is not an exact one. Some subjects and activities require more time than others, not because they are necessarily considered more valuable, but because their activities require more time in which to develop. Art, craft and games are examples. English and mathematics, however, have more time allocated them because they are considered more valuable to educational development, and the valuation placed on them is as strong in the infant school with its emphasis on number and language work as in the secondary school.

But time-tabled time has other effects, as Weston points out[3]. It may result in the fragmentation of pupils' educational experience:- eight different lessons in different parts of the school in addition to a variety of breaks. Weston argues that the small unit of time used as the time-table currency of many secondary schools not only results in the fragmentation of curricular experience but because of the complexity involved in apportioning the units among subjects and teachers it requires central control of time-tabling, leaving little or no flexibility in the use of time by teachers or subject departments. Weston argues for more 'open' time-tabling in the secondary school based on larger blocks of time with teachers responsible for how it is to be used, and with an encouragement to leave 'slack' or uncommitted time for activities that cannot be foreseen in advance. In those primary schools where time is used flexibly under an integrated day or 'open' classroom regime, it sometimes happens that time is not devoted to those subjects or activities thought to be marginal to the curriculum or over which the teacher is uncertain. Religious education, science and drama are examples[4].

The point to stress is that there are costs and benefits to be charged to any way of allocating time. Such costs and benefits affect the quality and range of curricular experience that are provided. There may also be other consequences. Teaching children to stop and start to a bell may be conditioning them to the workplace, the demands of institutions beyond the school. Some would argue[5] that the school is modelled on the capitalist factory, and within the school the allocation of time is not the servant of the curriculum but of the factory and the office. However, studies of the allocation of curricular time and of its effects in operation have been too few to yield firmly based generalizations about its overt and covert consequences.

Time and curricular intentions

As time in the curriculum is afforded to subjects and activities, it not only confers educational status on them, but also gives practical legitimacy to educational intentions. When English appears on the secondary school time-table or when a teacher in an open primary school fosters some language work with an individual or small group, this means that English (or language work) is worth spending teaching time on because it will . . . . . . and here each subject or activity has both its justifications and its claims to have practical effects. These are the educational objectives for which it is the vehicle: the skills, knowledge, attitudes and values which it seeks to realize. English, for example, makes claim to develop several distinctive modes of communication and understanding. The Bullock Report[6] speaks of expressive, poetic and transactional language as distinguishable modes of communication that it is the purpose of English in schools to develop. Science makes other claims: to be 'taught as a major human activity which explores the realm of human experience, maps it methodically but also imaginatively, and by disciplined speculation, creates a coherent system of knowledge'[7].

The claims of subjects vary with time and circumstance. As an illustration, history was taught to working-class children in the nineteenth century by means of stories of great men and women, its purpose being to foster two dispositions: love of country and the morality of service, both essential in a period of imperial power[8]. Today, now that imperial ambitions are frowned upon, history is taught with other ends in view, especially understanding the how and why of human behaviour in the past and its relationship to contemporary problems.

Not all subjects possess the chameleon-like qualities of history. Latin and Greek, for example, have sunk into the relative obscurity of minority subjects partly because the claim that the 'classics' provided a complete education could not be supported in a world of increasing technological sophistication, and partly because their claim to 'develop the intellect' was critically assessed[9] with the result that maths and science made equal claims in this respect. Today, it is generally acknowledged that many subjects because of their particular modes of picturing reality and of truth-seeking can make a contribution to the development of rationality[10].

At the secondary level a number of studies have been conducted into the objectives considered realizable through different curricular areas. Lewis[11] studies objectives in science, Wood[12] objectives in mathematics, Boardman[13] in geography, Thomas[14] in English literature and Holley[15] in sixth form physics and history. In Holley's work teachers of both subjects lay considerable stress on teaching for 'enjoyment of the subject' and for 'use of initiative' in understanding it. However, history teachers place much greater emphasis on making judgments (the ability to distinguish propaganda, prejudice and wishful thinking) than teachers of physics who prefer to stress a thorough understanding of the main principles of physics.

As with subjects at the secondary stage, activities in the primary school can be justified in a variety of ways. This is as true of the painting corner in the infant classroom as of project work with older juniors. Taylor and Holley[16] point to seven major areas to which the educational activities of the primary school claim to make a contribution:

Intellectual: First Level Cognitive Skills
Intellectual: Second Level Cognitive Skills
Socio-Moral: First Level Affective Skills

Socio-Moral: Second Level Affective Skills
Aesthetic Skills
Skills of Religious or Spiritual Awareness
Skills of Self-actualization

Organization of subject-matter
Curricular objectives may be pursued in practice not only through the allocation of time but also by the decision to treat subjects as discrete entities (geography, history, physics and so on) or as larger wholes (the humanities, the arts and the sciences). In the latter case subjects are integral to an area of study and what matters are usually the problems or the concepts rather than the specific information which is provided. In an integrated course such as that pioneered by the Humanities Curriculum Project, the behaviour of the teacher as ' neutral chairman' (see Chapter 5) is as important as the thematic organization of the subject matter around topics such as war, law and order, and relations between the sexes.

Another, distinguishable approach is one where disciplines are chosen not to be studied in themselves but for the light which they cast on a topic. The Schools Council Integrated Studies Project is an instance of this interdisciplinary approach[17].

The terms 'integration' and 'interdisciplinary' have been used loosely by a variety of writers, and much effort has been expended in discriminating what is meant by the terms[18]. It is clear that as dissatisfaction with the conventional curriculum has arisen so schools have explored alternative organizing principles on which to base their curricular policies. Calls for 'balance', 'breadth' and 'relevance' in the curriculum are other such principles. However, the work of Weston[19] suggests that only a minority of schools use the integration of subjects to any substantial extent. What is needed are studies of how schools come to adopt and implement policies based on integration or interdisciplinary work.

The option structure now practised in a wide range of secondary schools is a further way of organizing the curriculum, though generally it only applies to work in the fourth and fifth years. Subjects are grouped into areas, with English and mathematics being compulsory. Under guidance from their teachers pupils are required to select subjects from each broad area and so build an individual curriculum. In theory, pupils may make a free choice; in practice the more able the pupil is at school work, the more likely he is to be counselled into choosing an 'academic' curriculum. Few studies have been undertaken of the option system in operation. From those that have it is clear that the system fails to achieve anything like the individualized curriculum that was intended[20]. It tends to act more as a device for tracking the more and less able pupils into very different courses, though it also helps comprehensive schools more fully achieve one of their major aims, that of providing equality of educational opportunity for all their pupils.

Curricular Milieux
Schools' educational objectives are facilitated not only by the allocation of time and by the general organization of subject-matter but also by the curricular milieux created i.e. by the curricular ways of life to be followed in realizing schools' particular emphasis. These two factors — curricular emphasis and way of life — are two major dimensions of the operational curriculum. Put simply, schools tend to emphasise either pupils as individuals or as members of society. In the first case stress may be laid on intellectual autonomy, personal development, the cultivation of self-confidence, spontaneity and openness to experience — what has been termed 'self-actualization'[21]. In the second case schools emphasise instrumental and social skills and attitudes such as punctuality, respect for property and a readiness to accept social conventions. These differing emphases are not new. They have a long history in education best summed up in the concern for character development versus the concern for fitness for society.

Each emphasis calls for a particular setting for its achievement, a specific milieu in which it may be realized. Musgrove[22] speaks of the 'cloister' and the 'hearth'. The first setting is monastic, set apart from the world and subject to a 'higher' discipline — that of academic subjects or of the teacher as an authority. The second is within the world, focussing on the technical and moral problems of society, involved in its tensions, with the teacher as instructor in basic skills and friendly guide to the ways of the world.

Few schools in practice simply exhibit one combination of curricular emphasis and milieu. Most have to make some accommodation with the capabilities of their staff, with the aspirations of parents and pupils and with the underlying structure of society, each of which may lie in very different directions from those being pursued by the schools[23]. Nevertheless, at the level of curricular policy, schools through their heads and staff strive to create a certain curricular 'climate' in which teaching takes place. Of course, expediency can sometimes be the governing criterion rather than any thought out, justifiable curricular policy. Dickinson[24] found a tendency for this to be so in his study of headteachers' policy towards innovations in the secondary schools of one local authority.

Schemes of work and syllabuses
Whether or not schools have carefully considered, explicit curricular policies, they do at least have a notion of what ought to be going on when teaching is taking place. Such notions are often, though not always, conveyed through syllabuses and schemes of work.

In primary schools the importance of schemes of work has varied over time. Some years ago[25] they were considered restrictive of both pupils' and teachers' activities. Recently, however, many schools have begun to develop such schemes, but the latter are not always detailed, nor are they to be found in every primary school. Sometimes schemes are directly related to curriculum projects adopted by schools or to sets of text books or structured teaching materials used by particular classes. Sometimes the place of detailed formulations is taken by discussion at staff meetings or by incidental indicators of what should be taught gleaned from conversations among members of staff. There has been little or no research into how primary school teachers plan their curricula or into how they use their much prized professional autonomy which has expanded to fill the gap caused by the abolition of the eleven-plus and its restrictive influence on the curriculum[26].

At the secondary level syllabuses are not regarded highly by teachers. According to Taylor's study[27] they range from the perfunctory to the elaborate. They concentrate most on subject matter to be taught and least on how learning is to be evaluated. Aims to be served by the subject matter, content and teaching methods to be employed tend to play an intermediate role. However as Table 1 indicates there are marked variations among subject syllabuses. Despite variations it is clear that under the conventions of most class teaching, secondary teachers' main concern is to know what they have to teach. The same factor is of high priority when planning a course of study.

Table 1
Analysis of Content of Syllabuses: Average Percentage

Subject	Aims	Method	Content	Evaluation
English	14	30	51	5
Geography	6	12	81	1
Science	6	9	83	2

Schemes of work and syllabuses along with curricular aims and objectives form part of a means-ends model of education. Syllabuses tell the teacher what content to cover; objectives indicate what his coverage of content is to achieve. There are, however, other views which assert that what matters is the *quality* of curricular experience provided, not where it leads. This experience may lead in many directions for pupils depending on personal disposition and opportunity. Many art educators hold such a view[29] as do some advocates of primary education. For such educationists the purpose of the curriculum is to provide pupils with an opportunity to engage in educational encounters — in art to develop aesthetic ideas out of an encounter with materials; in the primary school to explore materials in an enriched environment and out of this exploration to discover ideas of language and number. For such a curriculum the availability of appropriate media and suitable materials is essential and flexibility in its use is critical.

Teaching and the operational curriculum

Sound curricular policies, time-tables that reflect them and schemes of work which support them are all part of the operational curriculum. They provide the enabling framework for the curricular life lived in classrooms, at the heart of which are teaching and learning. The acts of teaching are many and various. They include keeping order, organizing pupils and materials, interesting pupils in what they have to learn, providing activities through which to consolidate and exercise what has been learned, and assessing how well it has been learned. The way in which a teacher puts these acts together, articulates and paces them creates a curricular 'culture'. How he conceives his role and that of his pupils gives this culture a certain ambience or atmosphere. If, for example, the teacher closely directs the work that pupils are to do, gives them no scope to bring to it elements from their own background and determines how the work is to be done, then the classroom culture will be heavily authoritarian. Curricular life for the pupil will be teacher-directed, lived in the language of the teacher and at the pace he sets.

Studies in science teaching[30][31] have suggested that two dimensions of teaching style may be crucial in creating the culture of school science lessons. The first is the teacher's location along the science _____ teaching dimension, i.e. whether the teacher is more concerned with science than with teaching or vice versa. Along the second the teacher's location is in terms of his relationship with those he teaches, whether it is close or distant. As shown in Figure 10 these two dimensions may define the major parameters of the culture of science teaching, each quadrant representing a subtly different ambience in the teaching of science. For example, teachers in quadrant 1 tend to base their lessons much more on the content of science than on how the uninitiated come to understand scientific ideas because it is to science that they owe their major allegiance. They do, however, recognize that in their classes each pupil is different from the others, and they do make personal contact with most of them. In contrast to this emphasis on the structure of science, teachers in quadrants 2 and 3 are more concerned with how pupils learn science, though they differ among themselves in the degree of personal contact they make with the pupils.

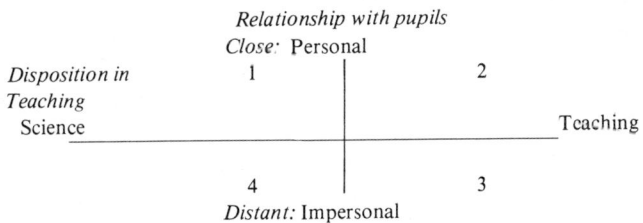

Figure 10 *Parameters of Science Teaching*

In practice the curricular culture of science teaching is less clear-cut than these examples suggest, though there is a tendency for teachers to develop, and feel at home with, one style of teaching, especially if they have not had the opportunity or the motivation to practise alternative styles. Teachers as much as pupils need a variety of curricular experience, if their learning is to show flexibility in use. What may be true of science teaching may not be true of teaching history or of teaching seven year olds in the primary school. Other dimensions may be more important in creating curricular cultures. Research and theorising are needed in this area, though Bennett[32] *et al.,* have made a beginning in their study of teaching styles adopted by teachers of upper junior pupils in North West England.

There are, however, other ways of describing the curricular culture of classrooms. Barnes[33], for example, uses a communications model and distinguishes between 'transmission' teachers and 'interpretation' teachers. The former believe that knowledge is contained in academic subjects, the content of which is verified against objective standards or criteria. These teachers judge what their pupils do in accordance with these criteria and see their job as one of correcting the pupils' work so as to bring it more and more into line with the standards of the subject. Pupils are regarded as novices, yet to be taught how to think and understand. This is similar to how the science teachers of quadrants 1 and 4 deal with class work. On the other hand, 'interpretation' teachers believe that what matters are pupils' abilities to organize thought and action so as to come to understand what they are experiencing as science or history. Pupils, they believe, do not start from ignorance but are knowers, yet to appreciate what criteria may be applied to give their understanding order and form. 'Interpretation' teachers see themselves, not as authorities, but as mediators of the interaction necessary to pupils' understanding of experience. Barnes' work, though speculative, is built on close, perceptive observation of the curricular life lived in classrooms. He sensitizes readers to qualitative aspects of the operational curriculum which he calls the 'effective' curriculum.

While Barnes uses a communications model to discriminate among the curricular cultures of classrooms, Weston, (in press) uses the concept of curriculum negotiation whereby teachers and pupils (as well as teachers and other teachers) work out a mutually acceptable programme and mode of teaching. The form which curriculum negotiation may take ranges from confrontation at one extreme to consultation at the other. With confrontation pupils may be *forced* to learn. With consultation they will *have a clear say* in what they learn and how they will learn it. It is rare for either extremes to apply. Rather, norms and rules for the negotiation of the curriculum are accepted by teachers and taught. Their nature, and this may vary with what is being taught, will characterize the curricular culture of classrooms.

Yet another way of viewing the way in which curricular culture of classrooms come about is in asking how teachers function to define the everyday realities of life in classrooms. At the conclusion of an interesting study of infant school classrooms King[34] says:

> 'Within this (everyday life of classrooms) they (teachers) also create other orders of reality: the story worlds of reading, the writing worlds of news and story, the world of number, of mathematics, and the world of conventional pictorial representation.' (p.166).

Each way of viewing the curricular culture of classrooms has something to recommend it. Yet none have captured in full the complex nature of the curriculum at the classroom level. Added to these views which focus on the explicit and observable nature of classroom activities are the studies of Jackson[35], Dreeben[36] and Keddie[37] who in their different ways contribute to an understanding of how teachers unwittingly create curricular climates in their classrooms. Their focus is on the unintended or 'hidden' side of classroom cultures. From his observations of elementary school teachers Jackson shows how the organization of the work of the classroom inures children to rules, regulations and routines. Keddie indicates how teachers frequently reject the inquiry-mindedness of their pupils in pursuit of their own plans for lessons and how they reinforce social-class differences through their classroom practice. Dreeben argues that the way teaching is organized introduces the young to certain salient norms of a democratic society, though it does not do so deliberately.

Much work remains to be done on how the curricular cultures of class-rooms develop and function, though quite clearly more than just the behaviour of teachers influences them. There are the forms of pupil grouping employed, the persistent individuality of pupils, the pressure of outside agencies, especially the examination boards, the multitude of practical constraints and the clamour of public opinion and 'great' debates[38]. Certainly curricular cultures are extremely complex, as is the evaluation of their processes and outcomes (see Chapter 7). What is taught seems to be *both* much less than is intended (at times only tenuously related to aims and objectives) *and* in some of its effects much more than is foreseen.

Further Reading

1. JACKSON, P. (1968). *Life in Classrooms.* New York, Holt Rinehart and Winston. This study of the curricular milieux of classrooms is a classic, empirical study. It is easy to read and suggests ways of looking at classroom life which promote new insights.

2. BARNES, D. (1976). *From Communication to Curriculum.* Harmondsworth, Penguin. In this book Barnes offers the reader a careful and systematic approach to the curriculum in operation. It contains a good mix of theory and fact, of evidence and assertion.

3. BENNETT, S. N., *et.al.,* (1976). *Teaching Styles and Pupil Progress.* London, Open Books. A provocative text based on research findings somewhat over-interpreted, but nevertheless raising issues of considerable importance for the understanding of the operational curriculum.

References and Notes
1. DAVIES, T. (1969). *School Organisation,* London, Pergamon Press.
2. WESTON, P. (1977). *Framework for the Curriculum,* Windsor, NFER Publishing Co.
3. WESTON, P. op cit.
4. This is a matter of current concern in primary schools employing an integrated approach to their work.
5. See for example, WHITTY, G., and YOUNG, M. (Eds.) (1976). *Explorations in the Politics of School Knowledge,* Driffield, Nafferton Books, and YOUNG, M., and WHITTY, G. (Eds.) (1977). *Society, State and Schooling,* Lewes Falmer Press.
6. Bullock Report, (1975). *A Language for Life,* London, HMSO.
7. Association of Science Education, (1965). *Science and Education;* Policy Statement, London, John Murray.
8. See the preface to CALCOTT, M. (1840). *Little Arthur's History of England,* London, John Murray.
9. SPEARMAN, C. (1927). *The Abilities of Man,* London, Methuen.
10. For example see the case made by HIRST, P., (1965). 'Liberal Education and the Nature of Knowledge' in *Philosophical Analysis and Education,* Archambault, R. (Ed.) London, Routledge and Kegan Paul, 113-138.
11. LEWIS, D. (1965). 'Objectives in the teaching of science', *Educational Research,* 7.3. 186-199.
12. WOOD, R. (1968). 'Objectives in the teaching of mathematics,' *Educational Research,* 10.2. 83-98.
13. BOARDMAN, D. (1974). 'Objectives and constraints in geographical fieldwork', *Journal of Curriculum Studies,* 6,2, 158-166.

14. THOMAS, R. (1978). 'Objectives and the teaching of literature', *Journal of Curriculum Studies,* Vol. 10, No.2, 113-122.
15. HOLLEY, B. (1974). *A-Level Syllabus Studies — History and Physics,* London, MacMillan Educational.
16. TAYLOR, P., and HOLLEY, B. (1975). 'A study of the emphasis given by teachers of different age-groups to aims in primary education', in *Aims, Influence and Change in the Primary School Curriculum,* Taylor, P. (Ed.) Windsor, NFER, 46-71.
17. This was the project developed at Keele University under the directorship of David Bolam whose paper published in 1971 (Integrating the curriculum: a case study in the humanities, *Paedagogica Europaea* 157-171) explains its philosophy.
18. For example, see PRING, R. (1973). 'Curriculum Integration' in Peters, R. (Ed.), *The Philosophy of Education,* Oxford, Oxford University Press, 123-149, and DEARDEN, R. (1976). *Problems in Primary Education,* London, Routledge and Kegan Paul.
19. WESTON, P., op cit.
20. WOODS, P. (1976). 'The myth of subject choice' *British Journal of Sociology,* 27,2, 130-149.
21. MASLOW, A. (1962). *Toward a Psychology of Being,* Princeton, Van Nostrand.
22. MUSGROVE, F. (1976). 'Marginality, education and the reconstruction of reality'. *Journal of Curriculum Studies,* 8,2, 101-110.
23. O'KEEFE, D. (1977). 'Towards a socio-economy of the curriculum', *Journal of Curriculum Studies,* Vol. 19, No.2, 101-110.
24. DICKINSON, N. (1975). 'The headteacher as innovator: a study of an English school district' in Reid, W. and Walker, D. (Eds.), *Case-Studies in Curriculum Change,* London, Routledge and Kegan Paul.
25. BEAUCHAMP, G., and BEAUCHAMP, E. (1972). *Comparative Analysis of Curriculum Systems,* Wilmette, Illinois, Kagg Press.
26. For consideration of 'autonomy' see BLYTH, W. (1965). *English Primary Education volumes I and II,* London, Routledge and Kegan Paul.
27. TAYLOR, P. (1970). *How Teachers Plan their Courses,* Slough, NFER.
28. TAYLOR, P. (1970). op cit.
29. EISNER, E. (Ed.) (1976). *The Arts, Human Development and Education,* Berkeley, McCutchan.
30. TAYLOR, P., CHRISTIE, T., and PLATTS, C. (1970). 'An exploratory study of science teachers' perceptions of effective teaching' *Educational Review,* 23,1, 19-32.
31. EGGLESTON, J., et. al., (1975). *A Science Teaching Observation Schedule,* London, MacMillan.
32. BENNETT, S. N., et. al., (1976). *Teaching Styles and Pupil Progress,* London, Open Books.
33. BARNES, D. (1976). *From Communication to Curriculum,* Harmondsworth, Penguin.
34. KING, R. (1978). 'Multiple realities and their reproduction in infants' classrooms', *Journal of Curriculum Studies,* Vol. 10, No.2, 159-168.
35. JACKSON, P. (1968). *Life in Classrooms,* New York, Holt Rinehart and

Winston.
36. DREEBEN, R. (1968). *On What in Learned in Schools,* New York, Addison Wesley.
37. KEDDIE, N. (1971). 'Classroom Knowledge' in Young, M. (Ed.)., *Knowledge and Control,* London, Collier Macmillan, 133-160.
38. See TAYLOR, P., *et. al.,* (1974). *Purpose, Power and Constraint in the Primary School Curriculum,* London, Macmillan.

Chapter 7

Curriculum Evaluation

Introduction

In the first chapter of this book (page 20) a systems model establishing the major activities and concerns of curriculum studies has been presented. Later chapters have dealt with various sub-systems. Here the focus is on curriculum evaluation — on those feedback loops in the systems model which involve judgments of various kinds related to the activities of curriculum design, development and transaction.

'Judgment' is the key term in discussion of curriculum evaluation. Judgments have to be made about what to evaluate, how and with what end in view. But before going into the what, how and why of evaluation one thing should be made clear. If the process of curriculum evaluation is to be understood, it is necessary to appreciate the close relationship between what is being evaluated and the form that the judgment takes.

A simple example will illustrate the point. Evaluating the skill of a marksman in a tournament requires that he is judged as to how well he can hit a target, at what distance and with what accuracy. Evaluating the quality of a work of art calls for judgment of a quite different kind. Failure to recognize that a different kind of judgment is required in each circumstance would, to say the least, lead to difficulties. Unfortunately, the field of curriculum evaluation has not been free from just such difficulties. This is because of the differing forms in which curriculum evaluation has been cast — because of the differing models or metaphors which have characterized it. This chapter seeks to describe views held about curriculum evaluation and secondly seeks to put these to work in providing a systematic map of the evaluation field.

The Scientific Model

The notion of 'education as a science' is relatively new. It stems from mid-nineteenth century sources and developed when psychology as an independent scientific discipline set itself apart from philosophy[1]. Central to the notion of the science of education, as it developed this present century, was the ability to measure the effects of education through the use of tests of achievement, attitude scales and interest inventories. Originally the measures were used as research tools to show in what degree education was distributed, and on what factors successful education or effective teaching depended. Later they came to be used as actual measures of educational success especially in the United States[2]. The development of such instruments has now reached a high degree of technical sophistication as a glance at any educational measurement textbook will show[3].

Along with the ability to apply measures to phenomena, science also requires that the process of measurement is *objective* i.e. independent of the observer. Science requires other things too — that the factors affecting the phenomena being studied should be strictly controlled so that the number of variables which account for a result are known and limited. Additionally, reproducibility or replication is required — other scientists should be able to produce the same results under the same conditions. The end point of applying scientific method is the discovery of the laws which govern natural phenomena, and it was the hope of discovering the 'laws of education' that was the inspiration behind the early advocacy of the scientific study of education.

Educational science was, however, only ever able to approximate to the canons of scientific method. Educational measuring instruments flourished, many with very satisfactory characteristics of objectivity and reliability but the strict control of variables was never possible, nor, except in limited instances, was exact replication. Instead, methods similar to those used in agriculture to study crop yields under differing conditions of soil, fertilizer and seed quality were employed[4]. Such methods called for the apportionment of the results to each of a number of variables, and this apportionment called for the use of complex statistical analysis. A knowledge of statistical methods, in fact, became essential for all who wished to make a scientific study of education.

Under such men as Thorndike[5] and Burt[6], a strong tradition of treating educational problems as largely scientific problems grew up and it was not surprising that when questions concerning the effectiveness of curricula were raised the approach to answering them was thought by some to lie within the methods of the science of education.

'Scientific' Curriculum Evaluation

'First define your educational objectives and secondly give them an operational (and preferably, behavioural) definition' have been crucial tenets of 'scientific' curriculum evaluation[7]. On them have been based blueprints for the construction of measuring instruments, the application of which has enabled curriculum evaluation to take place. The extent to which the objectives have been achieved has been accepted as a measure of the effectiveness of the curriculum. The process of ascertaining this measure of effectiveness has been termed the process of curriculum evaluation.

When concern for curriculum evaluation came to the fore in the late 1950's and early 1960's much work on defining objectives and giving them an operational definition (saying what pupils or students would be able to do, think or feel when they had achieved the objectives) had been done during the earlier vogue for programmed learning, and could be applied to curriculum evaluation[8]. In addition, Bloom and his colleagues[9] had provided a taxonomy of educational objectives in the cognitive domain and were busily engaged in developing a taxonomy of affective objectives. The curriculum evaluation model that developed was simplicity itself (see Figure 11). Its application, though widely advocated, turned out to be very far from simple.

Figure 11. *Elements of the Scientific Model of Curriculum Evaluation.*

The concern to evaluate the effectiveness of curricula coincided with a period of systematic curriculum development on a large scale. The concern to know whether curricula were effective in producing the desired results was paralleled by a concern to know whether the processes of curriculum development were operating as the developers and their sponsors intended. There began a 'product'-'process' controversy and the elaboration of an evaluation methodology differentiating *summative* or final (product) evaluation from *formative* or on-going (process) evaluation[11]. At this time, too, it was by no means clear what objectives would be accepted as valid, and by whom. Early studies showed that teachers and curriculum developers held as valid either different objectives or had different priorities within the same set of objectives.[12] It was also the case that certain prestigious figures opposed the objectives approach to curriculum evaluation from the start.[13]

In short, the scientific approach to curriculum evaluation could not be applied in its simplest form and led instead to a great deal of further work aimed either at elaborating and clarifying details of the scientific approach or at specifying more closely and carefully where and why it could be applied.

The specification of educational objectives remained the hinge on which the scientific model of curriculum evaluation depended. A good deal was written about objectives held to be valid in many areas of the curriculum and for various stages in education, and also about the relationship between educational aims and educational objectives. Much time and effort was also spent clarifying the nature of educational objectives, extending them in kind beyond cognitive, affective and psychomotor objectives to include objectives valid in curriculum areas such as the arts[14]. Efforts were also made at a rapprochement between 'scientific' and 'humanistic' curriculum developers, the former considering that education was about achieving given goals ('arriving'), the latter that education involved experiencing desirable states ('travelling'). The humanists accepted the validity of a curriculum involving a series of experiential objectives, each seen as 'an experience that is consummative or intrinsically valuable — the subject experiences it as directly interesting, satisfying, enjoyable'[15]. (p.22). They claimed that because much that was educational was open-ended and not geared to specific end-results, the behavioural objectives approach was concerned at most with instruction rather than with education. However, the humanists accepted that both instruction and education were part of schooling and that the inclusion of experiential objectives would redress the balance of the objectives model.

As implied earlier, there have been few direct applications of the scientific model of curriculum evaluation. These have been mainly, though not exclusively, in science and mathematics. One noteworthy English example is the Schools Council, Science 5-13 Project[16] which, in its *early* stages did attempt to *measure* the effectiveness of teaching methods by comparing outcomes with objectives. This direct measurement approach, however, was abandoned in the evaluation of later units piloted by the project team.

The arguments for and against the use of objectives as criteria for evaluation will continue. Their significance in this respect has been well put by Hogben[17]:

> 'Behavioural objectives certainly provide fairly clear instruction and evaluation guidelines within the restricted compass of simple instructional (training) models. Evaluation is a relatively straightforward task if one's sole concern is in assessing the extent to which students have mastered the particular behavioural objectives enunciated at the outset. If there is to be a one-to-one relationship between *unambiguous* statement of intent and student performance, then we certainly can, with comparative ease, assess student achievement of minimum essentials. However, this is *all* we can do. If we wish to assess and evaluate beyond this, different models are needed.' (p.47).

Much that has helped formulate the *scientific* approach to curriculum evaluation has had its origins in educational psychology. It has its counterpart within the so-called *rational* approach to curriculum planning which has developed from within educational philosophy[18]. Both share common premises, that the practice of education is intentional and that its effectiveness can only be *measured* by reference to observable behaviour. Though they differ in the language they use, they commend almost identical evaluation procedures.

The Decision-Making Model

An influential development of the scientific approach to curriculum evaluation was to extend it into a decision-making model. Cronbach[19], in an important paper, wrote of the necessity of 'intelligence' in making programme improvements, and meant by this the collection and evaluation of objective empirical data for curriculum decision-making. Stufflebeam[20] elaborated the decision-making model further. At the centre of the evaluation process (see Figure 12) is the decision-maker whose concern is to improve the curriculum. The process of evaluation is to supply the decision-maker with relevant empirical information about the curriculum in operation, and about its intended ends, i.e. what is to be achieved. These worthwhile ends or objectives are derived from the values implicit in the educational aims that the curriculum is to serve: a clarification of the value position to be adopted is thus seen as much a part of the evaluation process as that of collecting data. A further stage in the evaluation process is the development of an array of alternative ways (options) of achieving desired outcomes from among which the curriculum decision-maker may choose the one which seems best to fit the circumstances which he faces. The choice made is assumed to lead to the desired improvement.

Figure 12. *Decision-making model**

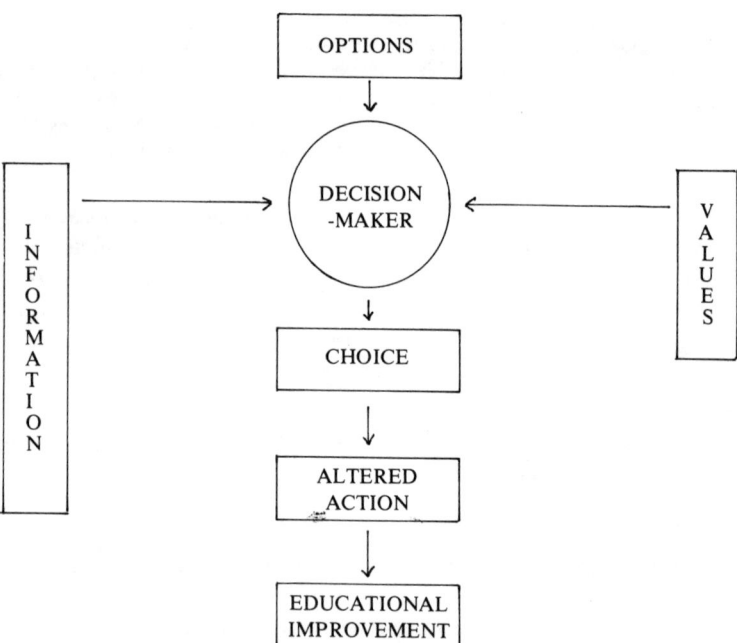

*This figure is adapted from Stufflebeam, D., *et al.* (1971). *Educational Evaluation and Decision-Making,* Itasca, Peacock, page 39.

Curriculum Evaluation

Others have produced variants of the decision-making model. Johnson[21], for example, using a logical tree approach, has laid out the process of evaluation as one of YES:NO decision points starting from 'Were intended out-comes achieved?' and working back to 'Was Curriculum selection valid?' Lutterodt[22] in a valuable synopsis of evaluation methodologies has provided a critical overview showing how information is deployed in the evaluation process.

A Change of Direction

As was pointed out earlier in this chapter, important curriculum scholars dissented from the scientific approach to curriculum evaluation based on behavioural objectives, and though failing to develop a fully-fledged alternative, nevertheless set going a controversy which continues today. There were, however, others who produced alternative models whose relationships to the scientific model could still be discerned. Notable among these was Stake[23] whose significant contribution was to demonstrate the many facets of the evaluation enterprise.

The basis of Stake's model lay in the two dimensions of *intents* and *observations,* (see Figure 13) and the three bodies of data — *antecedents, transactions* and *outcomes.* Evaluation required that data should be gathered on:

i) the antecedent intents i.e. what the curriculum developers had in mind in developing
ii) the intended transactions i.e. what events were intended to take place when a curriculum was transacted
iii) the intended outcomes i.e. what was to result from the intended curriculum — the skills and attitudes it was intended to develop
iv) the observed antecedents i.e. what classroom events were taking place before the new curriculum was implemented, especially the conditions of the teacher-pupil transactions
v) the observed transactions i.e. the actual activities engaged in when transacting the curriculum
vi) the observed outcomes i.e. the results actually achieved through the transacted curriculum

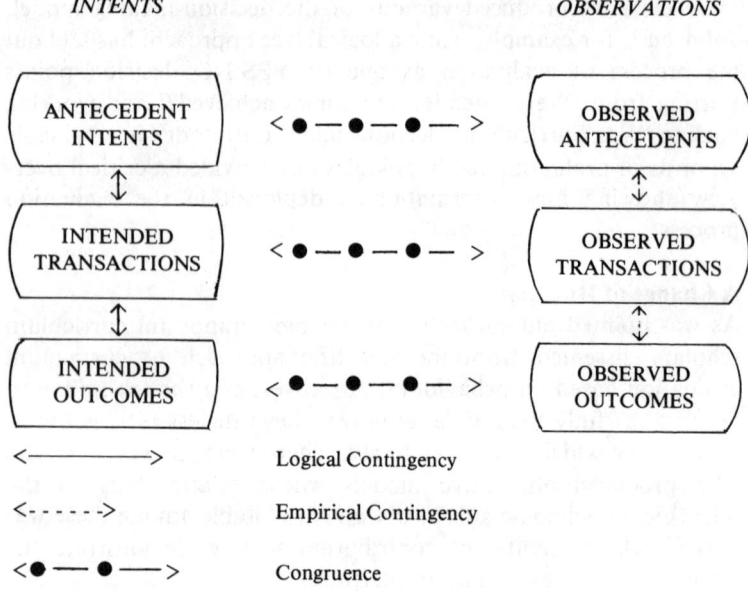

Figure 13. *Curriculum Evaluation Model (after R. Stake)**

*This figure is taken from Taylor, P., and Walton, J. (eds.) (1973). *The Curriculum: Research, Innovation and Change,* London, Ward Lock, page 94.

Stake argued that arising from the application of this model, data would have to be produced not only by educational measurement specialists but also by social and political scientists and historians who routinely study opinions, preferences, and values. But for him data gathering was not the end of evaluation; having clinically conducted his evaluation, the evaluator could not then wash his hands of it and leave others to judge its meaning and value. The evaluator's responsibility involved saying whether or not the curriculum was matching expectations (or intents).

Stake's contribution was to widen the evaluation perspective by drawing attention to the importance of both intentions and observations in the enterprise and by re-emphasizing judgment as the goal of evaluation, as Scriven[24] had also done. Even so, his approach was still heavily measurement-oriented, and theoretical. Of his early work, Westbury[25] said: 'Although these categories (i.e. those of Stake's model) are useful in a general sense, they are not close enough to curricular phenomena to be immediately helpful; they do not direct an evaluator precisely enough to the phenomena he is supposed to look at'.

The 'New' Evaluation

Westbury's comments were echoed by many who found the 'rational', 'scientific' approach to curriculum evaluation irrelevant to their concerns. Such critics were concerned more with the qualitative aspects of teacher-child-curriculum 'encounters' than with quantitative estimations of how far curricular goals had been achieved. The focus of attention was to be the 'diversity and complexity of the learning milieu'[26] — nothing less than the culture in which curricula were embedded. The stance of the evaluator was to be that of the anthropologist, concerned with description and interpretation rather than with measurement and prediction. To cast light, to illuminate, to portray, to be holistic, total, and comprehensive are terms used approvingly by the 'new' evaluators. This new approach to evaluation has been called 'hermeneutic' — concerned with understanding rather than with explanation. It aims to provide descriptions of learning processes and outcomes not in relation to prespecified criteria of success but in relation to how participants judge the educational worthwhileness of curricular experiences.

In providing their description the 'new evaluators' take a structuralist rather than an empiricist stance, taking the view that ideas and meaning matter more than events and facts. They seek to discover what meanings those engaged in the operational curriculum give to their curricular encounters and to search for an appropriate mode of reporting these meanings truthfully. What they appear to be seeking is value-free evaluation, a *ciné vérite* of curricular encounters.

In somewhat similar vein, Eisner[27], calls for 'criticism', 'disclosure' and 'connoisseurship'. 'Connoisseurship' involves teachers, evaluators and others in becoming much more fully aware of the range, richness and complexity of educational phenomena occurring within classrooms. Such awareness, Eisner argues, is already present but can be further refined and heightened. Criticism, however, is rather more than connoisseurship, though it includes it.

'The critic's task in each case is to provide a vivid rendering so that others might learn to see what transpires in that beehive of activity called the classroom'[28] (p.352).

In order to provide this disclosure, 'the educational critic employs a form of linguistic artistry replete with metaphor, contrast, redundancy and emphasis that captures some aspect of the quality and character of educational life' (p. 352).

Such criticism requires more than just the 'artful' use of language: the critic needs to recognize what is rejected or neglected as well as what is accepted when teachers use particular approaches in classrooms. Such a tradition of educational criticism, he suggests, has not been encouraged in the past, when the study of education has been dominated by 'scientific' approaches — 'An ounce of data, it seems, has been worth a pound of insight'[28] (p.354). The critic's function is to disclose, whilst the connoisseur's is to judge the qualities present in the objects of the critic's attention. His is an appreciative art, and for Eisner it is the appreciation of the many forms of educational excellence that is at the heart of evaluation.

The models of the 'new' evaluation thus draw on art as well as on anthropology for their informing metaphors. They reject the language and methods of the pure sciences and the technology of measurement, and because they have not yet fully developed their approach, nor have they published much by way of example[29], have tended to make evaluation an ideological issue; to be 'beyond the numbers game' is, it would seem, to be on the side of the angels. A more balanced view would be to appreciate just what strengths and weaknesses different models of evaluation possess, where they may be best applied, and how very limited remains our capacity to evaluate the curriculum in all its diversity and complexity, especially at the level of the educational system.

Evaluation at the Policy Level

Evaluation on a national scale becomes necessary from time to time because curricula are caught up in the practical enterprise of schooling, and society periodically expresses concern and disquiet about the standards being achieved by schools. Governments have available to them means of evaluating those systems of society for which they are responsible. The Royal Commissions and Committees of Enquiry are among the most commonly used means when what is sought is both a comprehensive overview and an appraisal as a basis for decision and action. Parts of the educational system have, from time to time, been the object of commissions and committees of enquiry. Most notable in recent years have been the enquiries set up under the Central Advisory Council for Education in England and Wales, each called upon to appraise the functioning of part of the educational system. The Crowther Committee[30] was concerned mainly with sixth form education, the Newsom Committee[31] with the education of the secondary school pupil of average and below average ability, and the Plowden Report[32] with primary education. Each committee not only looked into the organization of education for its specific age or ability group but also at the content of education — at the curriculum.

In each case the committee attempted to provide a comprehensive and dispassionate picture of the organization and content of their particular level of education, not only as they found it *but also as it might be*. It is in undertaking to do the latter that what they did became an evaluation, a matter, in this case, of appreciative judgment[33].

For example, if the work of the Plowden Committee is examined, much of the first volume is devoted to what goes on in primary schools, the factual basis of child development, both its physiology and psychology, the organization of schooling, and the content of the curriculum. To these factual descriptions are added the comments of the committee, commending, criticizing and selectively referring to the evidence either available from the empirical studies published in the Report's second volume or from witnesses interviewed by the committee. Also, the committee refer to primary schooling as they found it in other countries. What results from the committee's deliberations is both a considered view of the state of primary education including the curriculum *and* an indication of the direction it should or might take. The committee deals with facts, opinions, practicalities, and issues not yet settled, all informed by the values it wishes to promote. In balancing judgments of what is seen as the reality of primary education against what it believes to be of value in primary education the committee makes an appreciation, a considered judgment of where primary education is and the direction it should go.

In 1976 the call for 'a great debate' on education, on what should be taught in our schools, was a call for appreciative judgment, an evaluation of what had been happening in schools in relation to what might have been or ought to have been happening. In the *Annotated Agenda for Discussion*[34] standards of numeracy, the teaching of science and modern languages, the use of the mother tongue, assessment and the desirability of a common core curriculum were among matters itemized for discussion and debate. In such a debate judgments of reality (what is believed to be the case), judgments of interests (what issues are believed to be significant) and judgments of value (what is believed ought to be the case) came together in an exercise of appreciative judgment by many different groups — parents, employers and teachers. In short, what the Prime Minister called for in his Oxford speech[35] was an evaluation of salient curriculum issues at a time of national economic crisis. This last, the economic crisis, was the setting for the evaluation. It will doubtless affect the outcome. But all forms of curriculum evaluation have their settings; they are culture-bound not culture-free. In Parson's words[36], 'Our methods, concerns, and conceptualizations can be viewed, to an extent, as cultural artifacts; such a perspective may be of value in maintaining a critical awareness of new orthodoxies' (p.136).

Towards an Overview

If there is a central issue in curriculum evaluation, it is one of quantity versus quality, of measuring versus valuing. In the one case, judgment is based on the results of estimating the amount of an attribute, usually in relation to a standard, in the other, on the recognition of the intrinsic worth or estimable qualities present.

In the systems model of the curriculum (Figure 3, p. 20), evaluation was shown as the feedback loop from educated individuals to intended curricula and thence to the factors governing operational curricula. Curriculum evaluation has tended, and still tends, to be somewhat restrictively conceived, focusing overmuch on either the output (product) of operational curricula or on their processes to the neglect of the evaluation of what was antecedent to both, the process of curriculum development and the input to this process derived from conceptions and ideologies of education. In drawing attention to another aspect of evaluation, in this case, the congruence between the qualities inhering in intended curricula and the originating conceptions of education, Stake[37] has made a singular contribution. The work of Vickers[38] on how social

Curriculum Evaluation

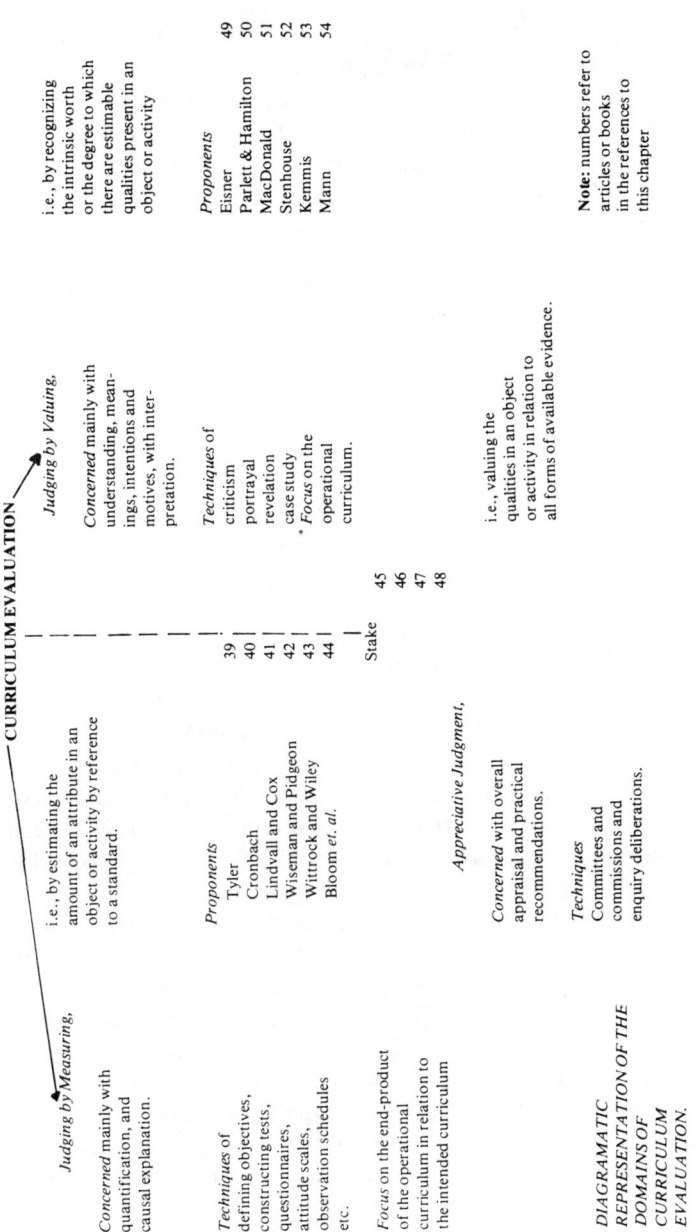

Figure 14. *The Scope of Curriculum Evaluation.*

judgments are made in practice has led to a realization that a larger form of curriculum evaluation, 'appreciation', has been neglected.

In Figure 14 (page 135) an attempt has been made to map the scope of curriculum evaluation in terms of distinguishable but interrelated kinds of judgement, and to indicate the techniques of each and their focus of attention. In addition, some indication of the proponents of each model or form of evaluation are listed, and some examples given.

The notion of judgment ties both styles of evaluation together. They are perhaps best thought of as opposite sides of the same coin, part of an organic unity rather than polar opposites. Their avowed ends are the same: the determination of the value to be placed on the curriculum.

The Politics of Evaluation

No chapter on curriculum evaluation could be complete without considering why curriculum evaluation is undertaken, and for what ends and for whose good its results are employed. So crucial to the process of schooling is the curriculum that all those who have an interest in it have also a concern for curriculum evaluation.

Systems of education are controlled by bureaucracies whose function is to administer them. Their function is *allocative* — to make available to schools resources in accountable ways. Their concern is with the efficient provision of a service, a basic part of which is to ensure that certain standards of education are achieved. To the administrator curriculum evaluation is a means through which he can monitor the system for which he is held responsible and so keep his policy-making informed.

But systems of education also serve clients — parents and pupils — who are concerned that young people develop valued skills, abilities and attitudes which will serve them in the many roles which they will be called on to perform. For them curriculum evaluation is a means for assessing whether what schools teach is likely to provide capabilities which they value. Their concerns would appear to be primarily with instrumental capabilities rather than with moral and social development[55]. What is taught in schools is estimated, then, by parents and young people in terms of values, with utility being a major criterion.

Those responsible for making the curriculum a practical reality have their perspective. Teachers and headteachers evaluate curricula not only in terms of the needs of the school and classroom in which the curriculum is to be transacted, but also in terms of defensible educational criteria, e.g. validity, significance, learnability[56].

Others concerned with schools and what is taught in them have different perspectives. HMI's, inspectors, educationists and educational researchers are concerned with specialized professional attributes of what is taught, to which they bring their own brand of expert critical appraisal. For inspectors in particular curriculum evaluation is a means whereby they judge whether what is being taught conforms to what, as experts in teaching certain subjects, or teaching at certain levels of schooling, they consider ought to be taught. It is as *technical* experts that they judge the transactions of the curriculum. In a strictly technical sense, curriculum evaluation is part of their *expertise,* though it may be a very unrefined form of evaluation built more out of intuition and expertise than out of a careful study of the methods and data they employ when making their judgments.

Finally, there is the wider society concerned with the distribution and accessibility of education to its citizenry. Society has a view through its political agencies of how education should be distributed. This view, or *political ideology,* will tend to determine the structure of the educational system and thus the shape of intended curricula. For governments and politicians curriculum evaluation serves to reflect the progress that is being made towards a desired distribution of one of society's goods and services, i.e., education.

Evaluation to monitor standards, to value, to test practicalities and estimate professional validity, to inspect and analyze, and to check progress may all be used as means of control. But whose control, if any, should be paramount? MacDonald[57] has raised this issue very directly, though somewhat contentiously, in describing the control of evaluation as:

i) *Bureaucratic,* i.e. evaluation to produce information for policy-makers
ii) *Autocratic,* i.e. evaluation undertaken by independent agencies such as the National Foundation for Educational Research or university scholars who are free to publish their results irrespective of the interests of policy-makers or

practitioners.
iii) *Democratic,* i.e. evaluation as a service to all who may claim an interest in what is taught in schools, and undertaken in a way which makes the information easily accessible to all concerned.

It is the last kind of evaluation that has been pioneered by the Humanities Project[58] and the National Development Project for Computer Assisted Learning.

It has been noted above that different groups of people take different stances toward evaluation, depending on their roles in the educational and social system. What MacDonald and others, notably Lortie[59] and House[60], have done is to highlight the issues which arise when the question of the control of evaluation is posed. Such issues are essentially political, concerned with the distribution and use of information and the power it brings with it. Understanding these issues is as much a part of understanding curriculum evaluation as a grasp of evaluation models and the techniques of evaluation.

This chapter has focused on curriculum evaluation — on those theories and methodologies developed to establish the value of curriculum proposals. The last chapter presents a more general overview of research and theories informing those concerns of curriculum studies outlined in chapter one and developed subsequently in the book.

Further reading
1. HAMILTON, D. (1976). *Curriculum Evaluation,* London, Open Books. This short introductory book raises most of the issues encountered in the field of curriculum evaluation. It is especially strong on the 'new wave' evaluation approach, and on the politics of evaluation. It is not difficult to read, and has a useful bibliography.

2. TAWNEY, D. (Ed.) (1976). *Curriculum Evaluation Today: Trends and Implications:* London. Macmillan Education for the Schools Council. This edited collection of articles on aspects of evaluation provides a very useful introduction to the subject. The articles by Harlen, Parlett and Hamilton, and MacDonald are especially worthy of attention.

3. BLOOM, B.S., et al. (1956). *Taxonomy of Educational Objectives: the classification of educational goals. Handbook I: Cognitive Domain,* London, Longmans.

4. KRATHWOHL, O., BLOOM, B. et al., (1974). *Taxonomy of Educational Objectives: Handbook II: Affective Domain.* London, Longmans. To be browsed through, if not read. The objectives approach to curriculum evaluation owes much to the work of Bloom and his colleagues. With the Handbooks should be read Gribble's article, 'Pandora's Box: The Affective Domain', in *Journal of Curriculum Studies,* 2,1, 11-24 which is a careful critique of an aspect of the objectives approach, the failure to recognize the value assumptions on which it stands.

Notes and References
1. See chapter 1 in THORNDIKE, R., and HAGEN, E. (1955). *Measurement in Evaluation and Psychology,* New York, John Wiley.
2. Witness to this is the rapid development of testing in American education.
3. For instance, see ANASTASI, A. (1976). *Psychological Testing,* New York, MacMillan.
4. See FISHER, R. (1949). *The Design of Experiments,* Edinburgh, Oliver and Boyd, for the roots of this measurement tradition.
5. Both the older and younger Thorndike's have been in this tradition. See THORNDIKE, E.L. (1906). *The Principles of Teaching,* New York; SEILER, A.G., and THORNDIKE, R. (1973). *Reading Comprehension in Fifteen Countries,* New York, John Wiley.
6. See, for example, BURT, C. (1923). *Handbook of Tests for Use in Schools,* London, King.
7. See chapter 4 on design.
8. See, for example, Mager's classic work, MAGER, R. (1962). *Preparing Instructional Objectives,* Palo Alto, Fearon Pub. Co.
9. BLOOM, B., et al. (1956). *Taxonomy of Educational Objectives: Handbook I: Cognitive Domain,* London, Longmans. KRATHWOHL, D., et al. (1964). *Taxonomy of Educational Objectives: Handbook II: Affective Domain,* London, Longmans.
10. See chapter 4 on design, especially section on objectives.
11. See SCRIVEN, M. (1967). 'The Methodology of Evaluation', in *Perspectives of Curriculum Evaluation,* (Ed.), Stake, R., AERA Monograph 1, Chicago, Rand McNally.
12. See TAYLOR, P., and MAQUIRE, J. (1966). 'A theoretical evaluation model', *Manitoba Journal of Educational Research,* 1,2, 12-13.
13. For example, Lawrence Stenhouse. See his 'Some Limitations of the Use of Objectives in Curriculum Research and Planning', (1970-71). *Paedagogica Europaea,* 73-83.
14. See EISNER, E. (1969). 'Instructional and Expressive Educational Objectives' in *Instructional Objectives,* (Ed.), Popham, J., AERA Monograph 3, Chicago, Rand McNally.
15. PRATT, D. (1976). 'Humanistic Goals and Behavioural Objectives: Towards a Synthesis', *Journal of Curriculum Studies,* vol. 8, no.1, May 1976, 15-26.

16. HARLEN, W. (1975). *Science 5-13: a Formative Evaluation*, London Macmillan Education. Another noteworthy example of 'scientific' evaluation is the IPI (individually prescribed instruction) programme developed at the Learning Research and Development Centre, University of Pittsburgh, and described in LINDVALL, C., and COX, R. (1970). *Evaluation as a Tool in Curriculum Development: the I.P.I. Evaluation Program*, AERA Monograph 5, Chicago, Rand McNally.
17. HOGBEN, D. (1972). 'The Behavioural Objectives Approach: Some Problems and Some Dangers', *Journal of Curriculum Studies*, vol. 4, no.1, 42-50.
18. See HIRST, P. (1974). *Knowledge and the Curriculum*, London, RKP.
19. CRONBACH, L. (1963). 'Course Improvement through Evaluation', *Teachers College Record*, 64, 672-83.
20. STUFFLEBEAM, D., et. al., (1971). *Educational Evaluation and Decision Making*, Itasca, Peacock.
21. JOHNSON, M. (1969). 'The translation of curriculum into instruction', *Journal of Curriculum Studies*, 1,2, 115-131.
22. LUTTERODT, S. (1975). 'A Systematic Approach to Curriculum Evaluation', *Journal of Curriculum Studies*, vol 7, no.2, 135-50.
23. STAKE, R. (1976). 'The Countenance of Educational Evaluation', *Teachers College Record*, vol. 68, no.7, 523-40.
24. SCRIVEN, M., op. cit.
25. WESTBURY, I. (1970). 'Curriculum Evaluation in Educational Evaluation': *Review of Educational Research*, vol. 40, no.2, 239-260.
26. PARLETT, M., and HAMILTON, D. (1972). *Evaluation as Illumination: a New Approach to the Study of Innovatory Programs*, Occasional Paper 9, Centre for Research in Educational Sciences, University of Edinburgh.
27. EISNER, E. (1975). 'The perceptive eye: toward the reformation of educational evaluation', invited address, American Educational Research Association meeting, Washington DC.
28. EISNER, E. (1977). 'On the Uses of Educational Connoisseurship and Criticism for Evaluating Classroom Life', *Teachers College Record*, vol. 78, no.3, 345-358.
29. Some British work along these lines includes the evaluation of the Humanities Curriculum Project (reported in MacDONALD, B. (1973). 'Humanities Curriculum Project', *Evaluation in Curriculum Development: Twelve Case Studies*, London, Macmillan), an investigation into education of the visually handicapped (reported in JAMIESON. M., et al., (1977). *Towards Integration: a Study of Blind and Partially-sighted Children in Ordinary Schools*, Slough, NFER) and Project PHI (reported in HAMILTON, D. (1976). *Curriculum Evaluation*, London, Open Books). The new approaches are thoroughly discussed in HAMILTON, D., JENKINS, D., MacDONALD, B., et. al., (1977). *Beyond the Numbers Game*, London, MacMillan.
30. CROWTHER, G. (1959). *15-18*, London, HMSO.
31. NEWSOM, J. (1963). *Half our Future*, London, HMSO.
32. PLOWDEN, B., (1967). *Children and Their Primary Schools*, London, HMSO.
33. VICKERS, G. (1968). *Value Systems and the Social Process*, London, Tavistock Publications, also VICKERS, G. (1965). *The Art of Judgment*, New

York, Basic Books, and VICKERS, G. (1973). 'Educational criteria for times of change', *Journal of Curriculum Studies,* vol. 5, no.1, 25-31.
34. DES, (1976). *Annotated Agenda for Discussion,* London, DES.
35. CALLAGHAN, J. (1976). Oxford Speech reported in *The Times,* 8 October.
36. PARSONS, C. (1976). 'The New Evaluation: a Cautionary Note', *Journal of Curriculum Studies,* vol. 8, no.2, 125-138.
37. STAKE, R. op. cit.
38. VICKERS, G. op. cit.
39. TYLER, R. (1949). *Basic Principles of Curriculum and Instruction,* Chicago, University of Chicago Press.
40. CRONBACH, L. op. cit.
41. LINDVALL, C. and COX, R., op. cit.
42. WISEMAN, S., and PIDGEON, D. (1970). *Curriculum Evaluation,* Slough, NFER.
43. WITTROCK, M., and WILEY, D.E. (1970). *The Evaluation of Instruction: Issues and Problems,* New York, Holt, Rinehart and Winston.
44. BLOOM, B., *et al.* (1971). *Handbook of Formative and Summative Evaluation of Student Learning,* New York, McGraw Hill.
45. STAKE, R., op. cit.
46. STAKE, R., (1970). 'Objectives, priorities and other judgment data' in Stake, R. (Ed.), Educational Evaluation, *Review of Educational Research,* 40,2, 181-212.
47. STAKE, R. (1974). 'Responsive evaluation' in *New Trends in Evaluation,* 35, 41-73.
48. STAKE, R. (1976). *The Measuring of Education,* Berkeley, McCutchan.
49. EISNER, E. (1975). op. cit.
50. PARLETT, and HAMILTON, D., op. cit.
51. MacDONALD, B. (1971). 'Briefing Decision-Makers', Internal Paper, Humanities Curriculum Project. See also HOUSE, E.R. (Ed.) (1973). *School Evaluation: the Politics and the Process,* Berkeley, McCutchan Publishing Co.
52. STENHOUSE, L. (1975). *An Introduction to Curriculum Research and Development,* London, Heinemann.
53. KEMMIS, S. (1978). 'Nomothetic and Idiographic approaches to curriculum evaluation', *Journal of Curriculum Studies,* vol. 10, no.1, 45-60
54. MANN, J.S. (1969). 'Curriculum criticism', *Teachers College Record,* vol. 71, 27-40.
55. See *Enquiry One,* op. cit.
57. MacDONALD, B. (1976). 'Evaluation and the Control of Education', in *Curriculum Evaluation Today: Trends and Implications,* (Ed.), Tawney D., London, MacMillan.
58. See Introduction by Barry MacDonald in ELLIOTT, J., and MacDONALD, B. (Eds.) (1975). *People in Classrooms,* Norwich, CARE Occ.Pub.
59. LORTIE, D. (1970). 'The Cracked Cake of Educational Custom', in Wittrock and Wiley, op. cit.
60. HOUSE, E. op. cit.

Chapter 8

Curriculum Theory and Research

Introduction

Curriculum theory is concerned with prescription, description and explanation. As a practical enterprise, the result of curriculum theorizing is to make recommendations as to what ought to be taught, how curricula *should* be designed, what dissemination strategies *should* be pursued, how time *should* be allocated among subjects and activities in school, and who *should* evaluate curricula and by what criteria. But it is also concerned with description and explanation: it describes and explains how curricula *are* designed, how dissemination *is* facilitated, and how time *is* allocated. In this sense curriculum theorizing is 'scientific'. In this chapter, both prescriptive and 'scientific' curriculum theorizing are considered, along with an outline of the kinds of research needed to provide them with an empirical base.

Prescriptive Curriculum Theory

Prescriptive curriculum theory aims to provide guidance for the design, development, implementation and transaction of curricula as well as provide justification for the adoption of the recommended practices (see for example, the prescriptive design models of Chapter Four). Guidance about what to teach, how to sequence subject matter, how to apportion teaching time, how to select suitable teaching methods and what appropriate teaching materials to employ may all be part and parcel of a prescriptive curriculum theory.

In providing such guidance prescriptive curriculum theorizing indicates the bases on which curricular decisions and choices are to be made. In other words, criteria of educational worthwhileness are made evident. Such criteria may, as was suggested in Chapter Two, be derived from many sources — from beliefs about the nature of society, or of man, or of knowledge or of teaching and learning.

From such beliefs can be erected claims that this or that *ought* to be taught. Plato[1], Rousseau[2], Dewey[3], Whitehead[4] and, latterly, Hirst[5] and Bruner[6] are some of the theorists who have made claims about what should be taught. So have practical educators such as Pestalozzi[7], Montessori[8], Thring[9], Kilpatrick[10] and, more recently, Charity James[11] and Sybil Marshall[12]. Men of affairs have also added their voices. C.P. Snow[13], civil servant, scientist and novelist, has been concerned to bridge the 'two cultures' of arts and science, and Arnold Weinstock Chairman of the General Electric Company, like businessmen before him, has expressed the view that what is taught should be based on a proper appreciation of the needs of industrial society. Prime Ministers, too, have been known to assert that schooling should be as much about the needs of society as about the needs of the individual and to start 'great' debates about such matters.

Whatever the basis in belief for determining what should be taught, some form of philosophizing is required in order to justify the worthwhileness of the choices made. This may involve social philosophy with notions such as 'justice' and 'order', or moral philosophy with ideas of 'right' and 'wrong', or again it may be epistemology concerned with knowledge and knowing. Whatever the philosophic system (Platonic, Kantian, existentialist, etc.) philosophy is essential to any adequate prescriptive curriculum theory, since is provides justification for asserting that this or that is worthwhile to teach and learn.

Some American curriculum theorists have attempted to play down, or even exclude, the role of philosophy in prescriptive curriculum theorizing. They claim that the curriculum theory is like theory in engineering — value-free, merely indicating means to a given end, which can itself be determined solely by empirical means. Thus, for example, by observing what tasks society needs to have done in order to function effectively; by assigning priority to the tasks and by assessing the skills involved, they allow the findings to determine what schools should teach[14]. It follows that given the end to be achieved, theory should concentrate on two matters: how the end is to be achieved and the evaluation of its achievement. The flaw in this approach is a simple one. Empirical means in themselves cannot decide the purposes that the curriculum is to achieve. Whatever *is* the case cannot logically determine what *should* be the case. Of course, it is possible in a given instance to accept that empirical evidence should be allowed to decide the purposes that the curriculum is to achieve. If this is done, it means making a judgment about what should determine the worthwhileness of the curriculum just as much as if the judgment is based on the value of initiating pupils into the cultural heritage or that of fostering personal autonomy.

But as part of prescriptive curriculum theorizing, philosophy is more than just the means for the justification of curriculum prescriptions. Once the principles for deciding what should be taught are clear, there comes the matter of selecting the content and the methods to be employed. This involves logical as well as psychological considerations. Philosophy has to consider means-ends questions[15], and to examine critically assumptions inevitably made about the nature of knowledge and the process of knowing.

Philosophy, however, is not likely to have the final say in the implementation of a prescribed curriculum. Other considerations such as those of practicality and expediency come into play. Curriculum theorists acknowledge that any curriculum prescription to be realized has to make its accommodation with the realities of school and classroom. To do this, the curriculum has to appeal, to persuade and, not least, to convince those who are to enact it. Here philosophy hands over to diplomacy and politics — to a process for reconciling conflicts of interests, power and practices. The result is usually some way from where the prescriptive theorizing began but may be a necessary outcome if the theorizing is not to be stillborn. 'Good' prescriptive theorizing makes plain its justifications, gives them appeal and a practical face, and comes to terms with the realities of educational practices. The failure of most prescriptive curriculum theorizing is that it cannot draw on dependable knowledge of how the curriculum functions. It lacks evidence provided by 'scientific' theorizing and empirical research. The collection and analysis of such evidence have not been major priorities during the last decade with its pressures for rapid solutions to curricular problems. Plenty of examples of prescriptive theorizing can be found in the literature on the curriculum[16], but empirical work is not nearly so evident.

'Scientific' Theory

'Scientific' curriculum theory is related to scientific theory in general, an outline of which may help to indicate the form such theorizing about the curriculum takes. A scientific theory offers a construction or model of reality based on an apprehension of the phenomena of the real world. Such a construction enables men to understand better the nature of that world, the laws which govern it and the limits within which the laws apply. Scientific theory also makes it possible under certain given circumstances to predict the results of the interaction of elements of the real world. However, it is the case that few scientific theories can *both* add to man's understanding of the world *and* enable him to predict the result of the interaction of its elements[17]. Newton's Laws of Motion concerning moving bodies is an example of how scientific theory predicts; they tell what will happen under given circumstances.

The construction or model of reality which a theory offers is a mental image, an *as if* picture of how the phenomena of experience may be economically organized. The models and constructs of scientific theory are a special kind of metaphor. This is clear from accounts of the discovery of scientific theories. For example, Kekule used the construct of a ring which he claimed came to him as he was dreaming, on which to base his theory of organic chemistry. The carbon ring is in fact crucial to an understanding of oil technology and the chemistry of organic matter. More recently, Crick and Watson used the construct of the double helix to represent DNA, the key to the inheritance of genetic characteristics.

Scientific theory based on an apprehension of empirical phenomena, serves also to put together the facts and the evidence for the phenomena to integrate and organize our knowledge of the physical world. Scientific theory does not determine the evidence, distort the facts or alter the phenomena. In this respect scientific theory is neutral. Its raw material is the world as experienced, not as imagined. Imagination plays a part in marshalling the evidence, not in adding to it, which it does, for example, in poetry and in art. Terms such as 'objective', 'independent', 'analytic', 'rigorous', 'dispassionate', 'clinical' and 'critical' convey the flavour of how the phenomena of the real world are dealt with in the development of scientific theory.

A third characteristic of scientific theory is that it usually only qualifies as such if it is stated in terms which allow for its falsification[18]. Clearly the process of falsification cannot come before there exists a theory to falsify, and just as clearly, there can be no theory without facts. But it is by no means self-evident that fact-finding must come before theory-building or vice versa. Sometimes it is the case that there are too few facts to make theorizing profitable, though as Schwab[19], has pointed out, this has not prevented people in the past from theorizing about the curriculum. Where facts are in short supply, fact-finding becomes of paramount importance. It also proves to be a frustrating endeavour because it is not clear what facts to seek and where to seek them. Theory functions as much to point the way to the facts as to facilitate an understanding of them. Theory-building puts itself at risk, for in seeking certain kinds of facts by means of which to support the theory, other facts may be found which refute it. In order to accommodate them, the theory may need to be reconstructed. Such is the dynamic of scientific theory-building.

One further point needs to be noted, not because it is a necessary attribute of a scientific theory but because failure to note it may lead to an assumption that in any scientific field of study there is *a* theory, *a* grand design. There is not; there are usually several theories operating at different levels. In physics, for example, there are theories about the origins of the universe and theories about the smallest parts of matter.

'Scientific' Curriculum Theory

What then are the characteristics of *'scientific'* curriculum theory? What, for example, are the empirical phenomena with which it deals? Walker[20] asserts that the phenomena include

> 'all those activities and enterprises in which curricula are planned, created, adopted, presented, experienced, criticized, attacked, defended, and evaluated, as well as the objects which may be part of a curriculum, such as text-books, apparatus and equipment, schedules, teachers' guides, and so on. In addition to these actual objects, events and processes the phenomena of curriculum can be, and in my judgment should be, interpreted to include the plans, intentions, hopes, fears, dreams and the like of agents such as teachers, students, and curriculum developers or policy-makers' (p.59).

What is clear from Walker's catalogue of curriculum phenomena is that there are different kinds of facts to be sought and evidence to be gathered. There are facts about the behaviour of relevant agents and agencies (see Chapter Three) as they plan, develop, enact or experience curricula. These facts about behaviour are on two levels: facts about what *is* done and facts about what is *intended, anticipated and sought after*.

There are facts about the characteristics of curricular artifacts — time-tables, syllabi, teachers' guides, text-books and teaching equipment including the design of classrooms, laboratories and other specialist facilities. These facts about artifacts may be crucial to an understanding of the curriculum, its design and operation. In a seminal article, Westbury[21], for example, has suggested that American teachers' traditional dependence on the text-book may well colour the characteristics of the operational curriculum. We in this country see the examination influencing the curriculum especially in the secondary school.

Facets about interactions and interrelations, which Walker does not explicitly note, are also important, as for example, the relationship between the timetable and the operational curriculum or between the selection of options in the secondary school and the quality of pupils' subsequent curricular experience. An understanding of the diffusion of new curricula is dependent on an appreciation of the relationship between what new curricula intend and the constraints, both human and physical, of the setting in which they are to be transacted. Facts about the three-fold interaction of teacher, child and curriculum are also of consequence, as illustrated by the work of Bellack[22] and Barnes[23].

Research is the means through which facts are gathered. As Dubin[24] remarks,

> 'It is symbolic that the activities of scientists are called research. Separated into parts, the activities of research are re-search, activities undertaken to repeat a search . . . The scientist is constantly concerned with re-searching the accepted conclusions of his field — the theoretical model he uses. He does the re-searching by probing for facts of the empirical world that falsify one or more predictions generated by his accepted conclusions of theoretical models. Then the re-searching turns to the construction of new theoretical models to take the place of those no longer able to make sense of the empirical world.' (p.7).

Re-searching the facts of the curriculum field is an essential first step in 'scientific' curriculum theory building. It is an activity which is crude since facts about the phenomena of the field have been little researched previously. It is crude too because most of the models of theories to guide the search for facts are primitive[25].

Curriculum Theory and Research

A notable exception is Goodlad and Richter's[26] conceptual system for the study of curriculum and instruction, which, though heavily dependent on the prescriptive Tyler rationale[27] does draw attention to the relationships between the knowledge available in a society for teaching (both 'funded knowledge' and 'conventional wisdom') and the values employed in a society for the selection of what should be taught. In particular, Goodlad and Richter raise the question of what agents and agencies are influential in determining what should be, and is, taught in educational institutions and what role they play in the process. This theoretical model has led Taylor[28] to embark on research into curricular influence systems and to extend this into studying constraints on the achievement of curricular intentions. In its turn Taylor's work has resulted in the development of descriptive models of curricular constraints, as illustrated in Figure 15.

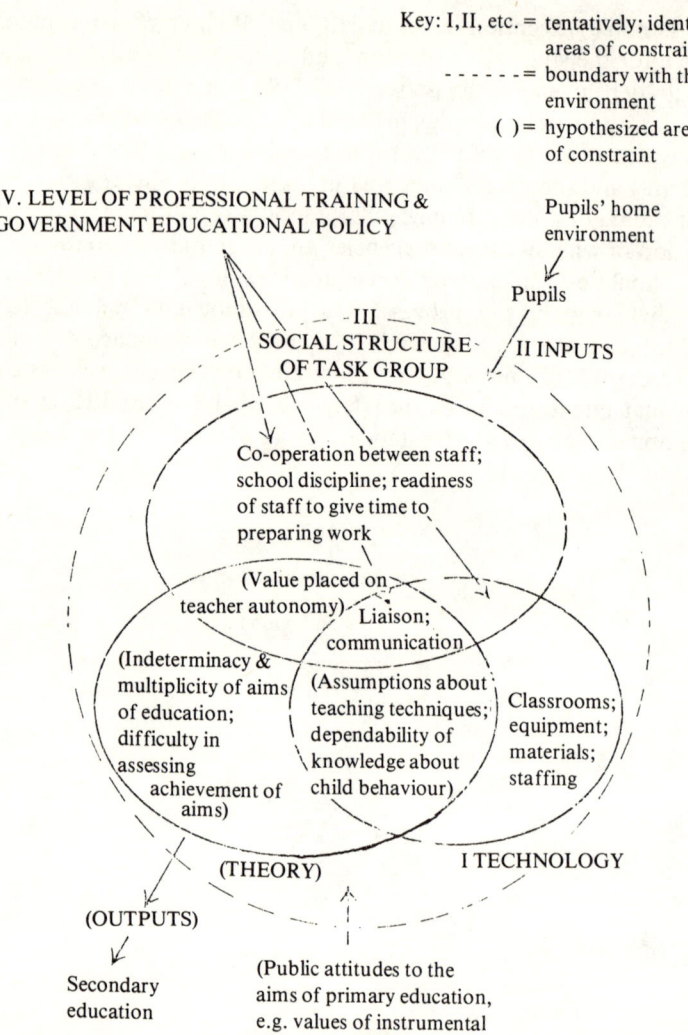

Figure 15. *Tentative schema of sources of constraint on the primary school's achievement of aims**

*This is taken from Taylor, P., *et. al.*, (1974). *Purpose, Power and Constraint in the Primary School Curriculum,* London, Macmillan Educational, page 36.

Goodlad and Richter take as the object of their theorizing the whole curriculum system as does Johnson[29]. Taylor in the work illustrated above focuses on more limited areas of the field seeking narrower generalizations about the curriculum system. Others have done the same. Barnes[30], for example, focuses attention on the operational curriculum through a communications model rooted in the primacy of language as the medium of education and uses this theoretical model to describe and explain how the curriculum is transacted under the different role-assumptions of teachers and taught. Like Taylor, Barnes draws on empirical data, though he tends to do so illustratively rather than systematically. Other examples include Shipman's[31] work on the adoption of innovation in schools associated with the Integrated Studies Project, Walker's[32] on deliberation in an art project, Tebbut's[33] on the diffusion of curriculum innovation, Cheverst's[34] on the language of educational discourse (in particular the role of the metaphor), Holley's[35] on syllabuses in history and physics, Taylor's[36] on how secondary teachers plan their courses, and Ashton's[37] on aims in primary education. Each example focuses on an aspect of the curriculum field seeking relevant facts and organizing them so as to illuminate our understanding of the phenomena experienced.

However, relative to theorizing in the natural sciences with their precision of measurement and power of prediction, 'scientific' curriculum theorizing is at an early stage of development. It is descriptive and has low predictive potential, though the latter is true of social science theorizing in general.[38] In the curriculum field this may be due to 'loose coupling' between the variables or elements in parts of the curriculum system[39, 40]. The concept of 'loose coupling' implies that the elements of a system are not necessarily 'logically' or tightly related to one another. For example, between the syllabus for a course of study (an intended curriculum) and the course as actually taught there may be considerable differences both in the subject matter covered and in the aims pursued, and for understandable reasons: teachers accommodate the intended curriculum not only to the pupils with whom they have to transact it but assimilate it to their own style. There is unlikely in the curriculum system to be the precise coupling between the elements that are found in the interaction, for example, of a chemical or engineering system.

In the present state of development a 'scientific' curriculum theory or an aspect of it either draws on facts concerning relevant curricular phenomena or points to facts to be discovered. It is mainly descriptive, though not ususally sufficiently powerful to exclude other possible descriptive interpretations of the same phenomena. It is because of this uncertainty of description that 'scientific' curriculum theory appears at times confused, contradictory and lacking the cumulative consolidation of theory in the natural sciences. 'Scientific' curriculum theory has little or no predictive power and does not lend itself to rigorous hypothesis-testing and thus to falsification along the lines of theorizing in the natural sciences. 'Scientific' curriculum theory is verifiable in the sense that the descriptions it provides of the phenomena and interrelationships of the curriculum system can be accepted to varying degrees as helpful in understanding more completely the behaviour of relevant people in the system or the characteristics of artifacts employed or the nature of the interactions and relationships among elements of the system.

Disputes about the helpfulness or otherwise of 'scientific' theorizing frequently hinge on the adequacy of the constructs through which curricular phenomena are transformed into images to aid understanding. Currently, and rightly, there is criticism[41] of mechanistic, causal models as means for representing curricular reality, and consequently there is an exploration of models based on literary criticism[42], drama[43], art appreciation[44] and diplomacy[45]. It has also been urged that to see in the term 'scientific' an implication that theorizing about the curriculum can be the same as theorizing about phenomena in physics is not only dangerous but also unwarranted.[46]

Certainly there are risks involved in using the term 'scientific' to characterize the development of descriptive curriculum theory, but some scientific procedures promise to be very helpful in this endeavour. Prominent among these are scientists' reliance on empirical research and their readiness to conjecture on the basis of evidence. 'Scientific' theorizing about the curriculum is slowly becoming established, though it has yet not fully avoided the pitfalls of all scientific theorizing: that of mistaking the model for the reality it represents.

Curriculum Research: Scale and Scope

Curriculum research is crucial to the well-being of the 'scientific' study of the curriculum and to the development of theory. The scale and scope of such research can be gauged by examining the systems model used in chapter One to map the field of curriculum studies (p.20). A number of broad areas of research can be derived from an examination of the various sub-systems, their interrelationships and the interaction of elements within them.

1. *Research into the processes of curriculum development, planning and design:* On the large scale, at what is termed the macro-level, this would include research into how the process is conceived and carried through; what relationships develop among the participants in the process; what strategies are employed, what constraints met; how policies evolve and how they become, or fail to become, effective in producing an intended curriculum. At the micro-level would be studies into the language used among participants, the meanings which they confer on such terms as a 'subject' or 'an educational activity', the evidence that is adduced in favour of one point of view or another, and the taken-for-granted assumptions which they make.

    Illustrative of research in this area is the work of Shipman[47] into a curriculum project, Walker[48] into the structure of curriculum deliberations, Davies and Ashton[49] into how teachers discuss aims and arrive at priorities among them and Ashton's *et. al.,*[50] study of the aims of primary education.

2. *Research into the outcomes or results of the curriculum development process* i.e. research into the structure of curriculum proposals, their units of construction, teachers' guides, curriculum materials and so on. Illustrative here is the work of Eraut[51] into means for analysing curriculum materials and that of Wyart on syllabus analysis[52].

3. *Research into the translation of the intended curriculum into the operational curriculum.* Here work would include the study of the relationships between curricular intentions and timetables and syllabuses, with particular attention being paid to the assumptions made about how pupils learn, what

interests and motivates them. Examples of such studies are those of Davies[53], Holley[54] and recently that of Weston[55] which examines the timetable for third year pupils in a hundred secondary schools.

4. *Research into the operational curriculum.* Here research would focus on what happens to the curriculum as it is transacted and given meaning in the interactions of teacher and taught. Of especial importance would be a study of how pupils come to understand what the curriculum in fact conveys, especially the knowledge and sentiments it helps build up. Barnes' work[56] and that of Bussis, Chittenden and Amarel[57] into how teachers understand the curriculum and give meaning to it through their teaching are illustrative of valuable studies of this curriculum sub-system. Elliott and Adelman's[58] research project into how primary and middle years teachers actually operate discovery-based teaching would fall into this category. No less important are studies of the so-called 'hidden curriculum', of the unintended learning fostered by the way the curriculum is handled and by the nature of the institutional setting in which it is transacted. Dreeben[59], Hargreaves[60] and Vallance[61] each provide distinctive perspectives on this topic, as does Jackson[62].

5. *Research into the 'results' of school curricula, into the achieved outcomes of curricular experiences.* Here are to be found issues of standards of learning, the degree of acquisition of worthwhile knowledge and dispositions. Both large-studies of the kind conducted by the International Association for the Evaluation of Educational Achievement (for example[63] the Association's study of science education in nineteen countries and of English as a foreign language in ten) and smaller scale studies are important. But it must be stressed that despite the large number of 'measures of achievement' studies there have been few which have thrown light on the role of the curriculum. A promising approach is to be found in the work of Duke[64] who closely questioned children about what they had learned and found that by far the greater part of their learning was of factual knowledge and far less was learned which involved a degree of cognitive complexity. Braithwaite[65]

also found in an examination of a social studies course that pupils were being taught a great deal that they already knew.

6. Research into the relationship between intention and achievement in different parts of the curriculum system — as 'evaluation', 'congruence' and 'appreciation'. Relevant studies here would include the work of Tawney[66] on technological studies, Harlen[67] on science curricula, MacDonald[68] on humanities teaching and computer-assisted learning, Hamilton[69] on open-plan schooling, Greig and Reid[70] on a curriculum development project in classics and Peaker's[71] work for the ILEA.

7. *Research into the relationship between the curriculum system and the wider economic, political, social and technological systems of society.* Such research would need in part to be historical. As in other matters, antecedent events may greatly affect contemporary curricular realities. But sociological studies are also relevant, as indicated by the work of scholars such as Bernstein[72], Bourdieu and Passeron[73], and Young and Whitty.[74]

The potential scope of curriculum research is considerable and is certainly not exhausted in the illustrations above. It will, however, not make a substantive contribution to an understanding of the curriculum — its development, operation and evaluation — if it is used merely to support one or other curriculum prescription. It will only contribute if it supports the careful, conscientious, laborious business of theory-building which in the final analysis may do no more than provide those in education with a more sensitised perspective than before[75]. Such an advance is not to be neglected. It could lead to a better management of curricular practices, though there can be no guarantee of this. There is, however, the satisfaction of seeking a way ahead and of unravelling some of the complexities involved in those seemingly simple questions: 'What should be taught and learned?' and 'What is taught and learned in schools?'

Further reading
1. DEWEY, J. (1902). *The Child and the Curriculum,* Chicago, Chicago University Press. This book is a classic of prescriptive curriculum theorizing by a philosopher who developed new assumptions on which to base curriculum decision-making. Equally valuable to read would be Plato on the education of the Philosopher Kings, or Rousseau on the education of Émile.

2. BARNES, D. (1976). *From Communication to Curriculum.* Harmondsworth, Penguin. In different vein this book attempts to weld theory and research into a new perspective on the operational curriculum. Its main concern is with the role of language in making the curriculum accessible to pupils. It urges that communication in the classroom be looked at as a matter of interpretation rather than transmission. It is a lucid and well argued contribution to curriculum theory.

3. STENHOUSE, L. (1975). *An Introduction to Curriculum Research and Development.* The work of Lawrence Stenhouse in the field of curriculum is well known and this book represents his most ambitious attempt so far to weld curriculum theory and research into a coherent system. It is not an easy book but readers of this chapter are recommended to read *Chapter 9 Towards a Research Model* and *Chapter 14 Problems in the Utilizations of Curriculum Research and Development.*

4. SHIPMAN, M. (1974). *Inside a Curriculum Project,* London, Methuen. This book is a good example of curriculum research. It is a case study of a project and its progress in securing a place in the schools. It is carefully written showing clearly how research and theory go hand in hand.

References and Notes
1. PLATO, (1955). *The republic,* trns. H. Lee, Harmondsworth. Penguin.
2. ROUSSEAU, J. (1911). *Emile,* London, J.M. Dent.
3. DEWEY, J. (1902). *The Child and the Curriculum,* Chicago, Chicago University Press. DEWEY, J. (1915). *The School and Society,* Chicago, Chicago University Press.
4. WHITEHEAD, A. (1929). *The Aims of Education,* New York, MacMillan Publishing Co.
5. HIRST, P. (1974). *Knowledge and the Curriculum,* London, Routledge and Kegan Paul.
6. BRUNER, J. (1960). *The Process of Education,* Cambridge, Mass. Harvard University Press.
7. PESTALOZZI, J. (1894). *How Gertrude Teaches her Children,* London, Allen and Unwin.
8. MONTESSORI, M. (1948). *The Discovery of the Child,* India, Kalakshetra Press.
9. THRING, E. (1886). *Education and the School,* Cambridge, MacMillan.
10. KILPATRICK, W. (1925). *Foundations of Method,* New York, MacMillan.

11. JAMES, C. (1968). *Young Lives at Stake,* Glasgow, Collins.
12. MARSHALL, S. (1966). *An Experiment in Education,* Cambridge, Cambridge University Press.
13. SNOW, C. (1959). *The Two Cultures and the Scientific Revolution,* Cambridge, Cambridge University Press.
14. BOBBITT, F. (1924). *How to Make a Curriculum,* Boston, Houghton Mifflin Co.
15. See, for example, SOCKETT, H. (1976). *Designing the Curriculum,* London, Open Books.
16. See, for example, LAWTON, D. (1973). *Social Change, Educational Theory and Curriculum Planning,* London, ULP. NICHOLLS, A., and H. (1972). *Developing a Curriculum,* London, Allen and Unwin. STENHOUSE, L., (1975). *An Introduction to Curriculum Research and Development,* London, Heinemann.
17. See DUBIN, R. (1969). *Theory Building,* New York, Free Press. Dubin is very clear and emphatic on this point.
18. POPPER, K. (1959). *The Logic of Scientific Discovery,* London, Hutchinson.
19. SCHWAB, J. (1969). 'The Practical: A Language for the Curriculum,' *School Review,* vol. 78, no.1, 1-23.
20. WALKER, D. (1973). 'What curriculum research?' *Journal of Curriculum Studies,* vol. 5, no.1, 58-72.
21. WESTBURY, I. (1973). 'Conventional classrooms, 'open' classrooms and the technology of teaching', *Journal of Curriculum Studies,* 5.2. 99-121.
22. BELLACK, A. (1966). *The Language of the Classroom,* New York, Teachers College Press.
23. BARNES, D. (1976). *From Communication to Curriculum,* Harmondsworth, Penguin.
24. DUBIN, R., op. cit.
25. See STENHOUSE, L., RUDDUCK, J., and MacDONALD, B. (1971). 'Problems in curriculum research', in *Curriculum Development: an international training seminar,* (Ed.) MacLure, J., OECD, Paris.
26. GOODLAD, J., and RICHTER, M. (1966). *The Development of a Conceptual System for Dealing with Problems of Curriculum and Instruction,* University of California, Los Angeles, Institute for Development of Educational Activities.
27. See Chapter 4 for discussion of the Tyler rationale and Goodlad's and Richter's elaboration of it.
28. TAYLOR, P., et. al., (1974). *Purpose, Power and Constraint in the Primary School Curriculum,* London, MacMillan Educational.
29. See JOHNSON, M. (1967). 'Definitions and models in curriculum theory', *Educational Theory,* 17, 127-140. and JOHNSON, M., (1969). 'The translation of curriculum into instruction', *Journal of Curriculum Studies,* vol. 1, no.2, 115-131.
30. BARNES, D. (1976). *op. cit.*
31. SHIPMAN, M. (1974). *Inside a Curriculum Project,* London, Methuen.
32. WALKER, D. (1975). 'Curriculum development in an art project', in Reid, W., and Walker, D. (Eds.) *Case Studies in Curriculum Change: Great Britain and the United States,* London, RKP, 91-135.

33. TEBBUTT, M. (1978). 'The growth and eventual impact of curriculum development projects in science and mathematics', *Journal of Curriculum Studies,* vol. 10, no.1, 61-73.
34. CHEVERST, W. (1972). 'The role of the metaphor in educational thought', *Journal of Curriculum Studies,* vol. 4, no.1, 71-82.
35. HOLLEY, B. (1974). *A-Level Syllabus Studies — History and Physics,* London, MacMillan Educational for the Schools Council.
36. TAYLOR, P. (1970). *How Teachers Plan their Courses,* Windsor, NFER Pub. Co.
37. ASHTON, P., et. al., (1975). *The Aims of Primary Education: a study of teachers' opinions,* London, Macmillan Educational.
38. DUBIN, R., op. cit.
39. WEICK, K. 'Educational organisations as loosely coupled systems', *Administrative Science Quarterly,* 21,3, 1-10.
40. WISE, A. (1970). 'Why educational policies often fail: the hyper-rationalization hypothesis', *Journal of Curriculum Studies,* 9,1, 31-42.
41. See PINAR, W. (Ed.), *Curriculum Theorizing: the Reconceptualists,* Berkeley, McCutchan.
42. WILLIS, G. (1975). 'Curriculum criticism and literary Criticism', *Journal of Curriculum Studies,* 7,1, 3-17.
43. ORAM, R., (1978). 'An action frame of reference as a register for curriculum discourse', *Journal of Curriculum Studies,* vol. 10, no.2, 135-149.
44. EISNER, E. (1977). 'On the uses of educational connoisseurship and criticism for evaluating classroom life, *Teachers College Record,* 78,3, 345-358.
45. SHAW, K. (1972). 'Curriculum decision-making in a college of education', *Journal of Curriculum Studies,* 4,1, 51-59.
46. JENKINS, D. (1973). 'The moving plates of curriculum theory' in Taylor, P., and Walton, J., (Eds.), *The Curriculum: Research, Innovation and Change,* London, Ward Lock Educational, 81-87.
47. SHIPMAN, M., op. cit.
48. WALKER, D. (1975). op. cit.
49. DAVIES, F., and ASHTON, P. (1975). 'Two analyses of teachers' discussions of aims in primary education', in Taylor, P. (Ed.), *Aims, Influence and Change in the Primary School Curriculum,* Windsor, NFER, 15-45.
50. ASHTON, P., *et.al.,* (1975). op. cit.
51. ERAUT, M. (1975). *The Analysis of Curriculum Materials,* Brighton, University of Sussex.
52. WYART, T., (1973). 'Syllabus Analysis', in Leedham, J., and Budgett, R., (Eds.), *Aspects of Educational Technology,* vol. VII, London, Pitman.
53. DAVIES, F. in ASHTON, P. *et al.,* op. cit.
54. HOLLEY, B., op. cit.
55. WESTON, P. (1977). *Framework for the Curriculum,* Windsor, NFER Publishing Co.
56. BARNES, D. (1976). op. cit.
57. BUSSIS, A., CHITTENDEN, E. and AMAREL, M. (1976). *Beyond Surface Curriculum,* Boulder, Colorado, Westview Press.
58. ELLIOTT, J., and ADELMAN, C. (1976). *Innovation at the classroom level,*

unit 28, E203, Curriculum Design and Development, Milton Keynes, Open University Press.
59. DREEBEN, R. (1976). 'The unwritten curriculum and its relation to values', *Journal of Curriculum Studies,* 8,2, 11-124.
60. HARGREAVES, D. (1978). 'Power and the paracurriculum', in Richards, C. (Ed.), *Power and the Curriculum,* Driffield, Nafferton Books.
61. VALLANCE, E. (1973). 'Hiding the hidden curriculum: an interpretation of the language of justification in nineteenth century educational reform', *Curriculum Theory Network,* 4,1, 5-22.
62. JACKSON, P. (1968). *Life in Classrooms,* New York, Holt-Rinehart.
63. COMBER, L., and KEEVES, J. (1973). *Science Education in Nineteen Countries,* Stockhold, Almquist and Wiksell. Also LEWIS, E., and MASSAD, C., (1975). *The Teaching of English in Ten Countries,* Stockholm, Almquist and Wiksell.
64. DUKE, D. (1977). 'Debriefing: a tool for curriculum research and teacher improvement', *Journal of Curriculum Studies.* vol. 9, no.2, 157-163.
65. BRAITHWAITE, R. (1972). 'N.S.W. Kindergarten children's knowledge of first grade Social Studies content prior to instruction', *Australian Journal of Education,* 16,3, 279-288.
66. TAWNEY, D. (1973). 'Project Technology' in *Evaluation in Curriculum Development: twelve case studies,* London, Macmillan Educational, 159-176., and DENNIEN, R., GUNN, S., SWINSWOOD, J., and TAWNEY, D. (1973). 'Devising evaluation instruments for technological problem-solving', *Journal of Curriculum Studies,* 5,2, 122-132.
67. HARLEN, W. (1975). *Science 5-13: a formative evaluation,* London, Macmillan Educational.
68. MacDONALD, B. (1973). 'Humanities Curriculum Project' in *Evaluation in Curriculum Development: twelve case studies,* London, Macmillan Educational, 80-90, and papers in HAMINGSON, D. (Ed.), (1973). *Towards Judgment,* Norwich, Centre for Applied Research in Education.
69. HAMILTON, D. (1977). *In Search of Structure,* Edinburgh, Hodder and Stoughton.
70. GRIEG, C., and REID, W. (in press), 'Ideals and realities in curriculum development, a case study of the Cambridge School Classics Project', *Journal of Curriculum Studies.*
71. PEAKER, G. (1975). *An Empirical Study of Education in Twenty-One Countries,* Stockholm, Almquist and Wiksell.
72. For example, BERNSTEIN, B. (1971). 'On the classification and framing of educational knowledge', in Young, M., (Ed.), *Knowledge and Control,* London, Collier-Macmillan.
73. BOURDIEU, P., and PASSERON, J.C. (1977). *Reproduction in Education, Society and Culture,* London, Sage Publications.
74. YOUNG, M., and WHITTY, C. (Eds.) (1977). *Society, State and Schooling,* Lewes, Falmer Press, and WHITTY, G., and YOUNG, M. (Eds.) (1976). *Explorations in the politics of school knowledge,* Driffield, Nafferton Books.
75. DIXON, K. (1973). *Sociological Theory,* London, Routledge and Kegan Paul.

Index

Adelman, C., 88, 154
Adoption of innovations 95f
  strategies for 96
Advisers, role in curriculum
  development 59
Aesthetic education 70, 82, 151
Agencies of curriculum development,
  52-5
Aims of Primary Education Project,
  80, 151
Amarel M., 154
Appreciation in curriculum
  evaluation 18, 133-34, 135
Aquinas T., 36
Art and Craft Education 8-13
  Project, 91
Ashton P., 86, 151, 153
Augustine, 28, 35, 36

Barnes, D., 118, 148, 151, 154
Bassett G., 51
Bates, A., 87
B.B.C., its role in curriculum
  development 58
Behavioural objectives, 64, 126
  criticisms of 69f
Beliefs on nature of education 14,
  27f
Bellack, A, 148
Bennett, S. N., 89, 100, 117
Bernstein, B., 32-3, 38, 155
Bernstein, M., 99
Bloom, B., 65-66
Blyth, W., 81, 101
Boardman, D., 112
Bourdieu, P., 155
Braithwaite, R., 154
Broudy, H., 32
Brown, M., 100
Bruner, J., 37, 144
Burstall, C., 57
Burt, C., 124
Bussis, A., 154

Calvin, J., 36
Carlson, R., 98-99
Central Advisory Councils for
  Education, 56, 133
Central government, influence of on
  curriculum, 57

Centre for Applied Research in
  Education, 56
Centre-periphery model of
  dissemination, 92
Change-agents, 88, 96
Cheverst, W., 151
Childhood nature of, 35f
Chin, R., 96
China, 29
Chittenden, E., 154
Classics, teaching of, 112
Classroom, cultures of, 116f
Colleges of education, role in
  innovation, 59
Congruence, 18, 20
Connoisseurship, 132
Constraints on curriculum, 150
Corwin, R., 99
Cox, R., 135
Cronbach, L., 127, 135
Crowther Report, 133
Culture and the curriculum, 14,
  25-26
Curriculum — compulsory 33
  conceptions of 14f
  core 34
  definitions of 11
  deliberation 82
  judgment 123
  curriculum theory, 19-21, 142f
  systems model, 19-20

Davies, F., 153, 154
Davies, I., 40
Davies, T., 110
Deliberation in curriculum
  development, 82
Department of Education and
  Science, 56
Descriptive curriculum theory, 145f
Design of curriculum 63f
  objectives model in, 63f, 116
  process model in, 72f
  situational model in, 74f, 88
Development of curriculum,
  agencies in, 52f
  assumptions underlying, 50-2
  definition of, 48
  and innovation, 48
  in schools, 85-9

Index

problem-solving model in, 87
R.D. and D. model in, 80, 87
Dewey, J., 29, 144
Dickinson, N., 101, 115
Diffusion of curricula, 91
Dissemination of curricula, 91
Dissemination of curricula, 92f
  models of, 92-3
Dreeben, R., 119, 154
Dubin, R., 148
Duke, D., 154

Eisner, E., 70, 71, 82, 131-2, 135
Elliott, J., 88, 154
Ends of education, 27-30
Eraut, M., 51, 88, 153
Evaluation of curricula 17, 123f
  appreciation in, 133
  decision-making model, 127-9
  formative evaluation, 126
  new models for, 131f
  politics of, 136-8
  scientific models of, 125-7
  Stake's model of, 129
  summative evaluation, 126
Evans, P., 88
Examination Boards, influence of, 57

Ford Teaching Project, 88

Geography for the Young School
  Leaver Project, 59
Giaquinta, J., 99
'Good practice' projects, 85
Goodlad, J., 67, 149, 151
Gray, K., 83
Great Debate, 41, 57, 119, 133, 144
Green Paper 1977, 18
Greig, C., 155
Groarke, M., 88
Gronlund, N., 64
Gross, N., 99

Hamilton, D., 135, 155
Harding, J., 101
Harlen, W., 155
Hargreaves, 154
Havelock, R., 87
Headteachers', role in innovation, 100
Hidden curriculum, 12, 119, 154
Hirst, P., 31-2, 71, 144
History, teaching of, 112
History, Geography, Social Science
  8-13 Project, 80, 85, 91
H.M.I., 56, 136
Hogben, D., 127
Holley, B., 112-3, 151, 154
Holly, D., 30
House, E., 92, 138

Hoyle, E., 101
Humanities Curriculum Project, 15,
  59, 73, 81, 85, 90, 93, 118, 137

I.B.A., role in curriculum
  development, 58
Ideologies 14, 38f
  definition of, 39
  conservative, 30, 40
  democratic, 41
  group interest, 40
  and power, 42
  radical, 30
  romantic, 41
  revisionist, 41
Innovation, 15, 79f
  take-up of, 99
  in U.S.A., 82, 92, 98
Integration and the curriculum, 113
Integrated Studies Project, 83, 85,
  91, 113, 151
Intended Curriculum, 16, 17, 153-4

Jackson, P., 86, 119, 154
James, C., 144
Jensen, A., 36
Johnson, M., 48, 129, 151
Judgment in evaluation, 123, 136
  appreciative, 133

Keddie, N., 119
Keith, P., 99
Kelly, P., 93, 101
Kemmis, S., 135
Kerr, J., 68
Kilpatrick, W., 144
King, R., 119
Knowledge, boundaries within, 32
  commonsense, 35
  distribution of, 26
  forms of, 31-2
  high status, 34
  objective, 31
  relative, 31
  transmission of, 26

Language, modes of, 111
L.E.A.'s, role of advisers, 59
  role in dissemination, 93
  role in evaluation, 136
Lewis, D., 112
Lindvall, C., 135
Lortie, D., 138
Lutterodt, S., 129

MacDonald, B., 85, 99, 101, 135,
  137, 138, 155
MacDonald, G., 97
MacMullen, T., 97
M.A.C.O.S., 81

Mager, R., 64
Mann, D., 98
Mann, J., 135
Marshall, S., 144
Means-end model, of the curriculum, 13
  in curriculum planning, 64, 116, 145
Merritt, J., 68
Metaphors in curriculum, 39, 41, 146, 151
Middle Years of Schooling Project, 85
Mill, J., 35
Montessori, M., 144
Mort, P., 98
Musgrove, F., 114

Newsom Report, 133
N.F.E.R., 56
Nicodemus, R., 101
North-West Regional Curriculum Development Project, 80, 83
Nuffield Foundation sponsored projects, 15, 56, 80, 91
Nuffield Junior Science, 81
Nyerere, J., 29

Oakeshott, M., 30
Objectives, behavioural, 64-5, 80
  criticism of, 69f
  expressive, 71
  in evaluation 126-7
  taxonomy of, 65-6, 112
Operational curriculum, 16, 109f
Organizational structure and innovation, 97
Organization of school time, 109f
Owen, J., 48, 58

Parlett, M., 135
Parsons, C., 134
Passeron, J., 155
Peaker, G., 155
Pestalozzi, J., 144
Peters, R., 33
Phenix, P., 32
Piaget, J., 37
Pidgeon, D., 135
Planning of the curriculum, 64f
  in primary schools, 86, 115
  in secondary schools, 68, 87-88, 115
  research into, 153
Planning, rational model, 64f, 80
  process model, 72f, 81
  situational model, 74f
Platform, 82-3
Plato, 11, 27, 35, 36, 144
Plowden Report, 14, 18, 133

Politics of evaluation, 136-8
Popham, J., 64, 71
Power and curriculum, 42
Prescriptive curriculum theory, 143f
Principles of procedure, 73
Professional autonomy, 51
Projects, 51, 79, 83f
Publishers, role of, 58

Rational planning model, 64f, 127
  criticisms of, 68f
R.D. and D. model in curriculum, 80
Reid, W., 155
Religious education, 34
Richards, C., 51
Richardson, E., 83
Richter, M., 67, 149, 151
Rogers, E., 97
Rousseau, J., 28-9, 144
Rudd, W., 101
Rudduck, J., 85, 93, 94-5, 101

S.A.F.A.R.I. Project, 100
Schemes of work, 115, 153
Schon, D., 92
School-based curriculum development, 59, 87f
School, organization of, 110
Schools Council, 15, 55, 79, 89
Science, influence on curriculum 10, 124
  objectives of, 70
  teaching, 117
Science 5-13 Project, 65, 80, 127
'Scientific' curriculum theory 145f
  evaluation of education, 124f
Scriven, M., 130
Shipman, M., 83, 85, 101, 151
Shoemaker, E., 97
Situational model of planning, 74f, 81
Skilbeck, M., 74-5, 76, 88
Smith, L., 99
Smith, M., 100
Snow, C., 144
Social interaction model of dissemination, 92
Social studies curriculum, 10, 85
Social Studies 8-13 Project, 85
Sockett, H., 70, 75-6, 81
Stake, R., 129-30, 134, 135
Stenhouse, L., 60, 70, 72-4, 81, 88, 135
Stufflebeam, D., 127-28
Subject associations, 57
Systems model of the curriculum, 19-20

Taba, H., 67
Take-up of innovations, 99-100

Index

Tanzania, curricula in 29
Tawney, D., 155
Taylor, P.H., 68, 73, 86-7, 89, 112-3, 115-6, 149-50, 151
Taylor, W., 31
Technology project, 90
Teachers' centres, 58-9
Teachers as cultural agents, 26
Teaching and innovation, 97
  styles, 117-20
  two models of, 37-8, 114
Tebbutt, M., 151
Thomas, R., 112
Thorndike, E., 124
Thring, E., 144
Time, in curriculum organization, 109
Timetables, 110, 153
Tyler, R., 63-4, 66, 67, 68, 80, 135, 149

Ungoed-Thomas, J., 94

Vallance, E., 154
Values in the curriculum, 17, 82
Vickers, G., 134-5

Walker, D., 82, 83, 84, 147, 151, 153
Walker, R., 99, 101, 148
Weinstock, A., 144
Westbury, I., 130-1, 148
Weston, P., 110, 113, 118, 154
Wheeler, D., 67
White, J., 33
Whitehead, A., 144
Whitty, G., 155
Wiley, D., 135
Wiseman, S., 135
Wittrock, M., 135
Wood, R., 112
Wyart, T., 153

Yegge, J., 99
Young, M., 56, 155